Starving the Exam Stress Gremlin

A Cognitive Behavioural Therapy Workbook on Managing Exam Stress for Young People

Kate Collins-Donnelly

Jessica Kingsley *Publishers*
London and Philadelphia

First published in 2018
by Jessica Kingsley Publishers
73 Collier Street
London N1 9BE, UK
and
400 Market Street, Suite 400
Philadelphia, PA 19106, USA

www.jkp.com

Library of Congress Cataloging in Publication Data
A CIP catalog record for this book is available from the Library of Congress

British Library Cataloguing in Publication Data
A CIP catalogue record for this book is available from the British Library

ISBN 978 1 84905 698 4
eISBN 978 1 78450 214 0

Printed and bound in Great Britain

'*Starving the Exam Stress Gremlin* meets a very real need given the increasing academic pressures on young people today. While there is plenty of advice out there about revision techniques, in my opinion, there is nothing so accessible, clear and well-researched about exam stress, its causes and ways to tackle it as this innovative workbook. My favourite thing is that *Starving the Exam Stress Gremlin* hands control back to young people – control over their own response to their exams – taking them on a journey from understanding to action. Unique, practical, humorous and warm; I would certainly recommend it to anyone whose exam stress is a barrier to success.'

– *Claire Tasker, Headteacher, High Storrs School, Sheffield*

'Another fantastic addition to the 'Starving the Gremlin' series. This series has been truly transformational – both for our young people and the adults who work with them. Kate has a way of making the most complex concepts of cognitive behavioural therapy understandable to all through a mix of written explanation, examples and creative illustration. Instantly usable, this latest workbook will be an invaluable resource for young people facing exams and for the adults helping them to prepare. A must read for anyone facing this situation or for those wanting to learn more about cognitive behavioural therapy in general and its impact on our emotions and behaviours.'

– *Rob Barraclough, Headteacher,*
St. Joseph's Catholic Primary School, Dewsbury

'In today's exam-led system, teaching the content of this unique book is, in my opinion, as important as teaching the subject content of the exam itself in order to create the positive conditions needed for mental wellbeing *and* academic success. Parents and professionals can also use the book's supportive techniques and reassuring phrases to encourage resilience, determination and a positive 'can do' approach from their child. As an emergency go-to or a step by step guide delivered over a period of time, this highly interactive workbook provides strategies to empower and take back control of the feelings which can challenge our ability to shine under test conditions. This book's accessible format transforms the science behind our 'Exam Stress Gremlins' into simple 'so what can I do about it?' guidance for lifelong success! Combining this with its easy to read style and use of stories and cartoons makes *Starving the Exam Stress Gremlin* a vital and memorable read!'

– *Vanessa Langley, Executive Headteacher, Gleadless*
and Arbourthorne Primary Federation, Sheffield

by the same author

Starving the Anxiety Gremlin
A Cognitive Behavioural Therapy Workbook on Anxiety Management for Young People
Kate Collins-Donnelly
ISBN 978 1 84905 341 9
eISBN 978 0 85700 673 8

Starving the Stress Gremlin
A Cognitive Behavioural Therapy Workbook on Stress Management for Young People
Kate Collins-Donnelly
ISBN 978 1 84905 340 2
eISBN 978 0 85700 672 1

Starving the Anger Gremlin
A Cognitive Behavioural Therapy Workbook on Anger Management for Young People
Kate Collins-Donnelly
ISBN 978 1 84905 286 3
eISBN 978 0 85700 621 9

Banish Your Body Image Thief
A Cognitive Behavioural Therapy Workbook on Building Positive Body Image for Young People
Kate Collins-Donnelly
ISBN 978 1 84905 463 8
eISBN 978 0 85700 842 8

Banish Your Self-Esteem Thief
A Cognitive Behavioural Therapy Workbook on Building Positive Self-Esteem for Young People
Kate Collins-Donnelly
ISBN 978 1 84905 462 1
eISBN 978 0 85700 841 1

of related interest

The Healthy Coping Colouring Book and Journal
Creative Activities to Help Manage Stress, Anxiety and Other Big Feelings
Pooky Knightsmith
Illustrated by Emily Hamilton
ISBN 978 1 78592 139 1
eISBN 978 1 78450 405 2

Set for Success
Activities for Teaching Emotional, Social and Organisational Skills
Josie Santomauro and Margaret Anne Carter
Illustrated by Carla Marino
ISBN 978 1 84905 058 6
eISBN 978 0 85700 244 0

Acknowledgements

First, I would like to thank all the young people who had the confidence and courage to share their stories in this book in order to help others, as well as the young people who have given me their thoughts and feedback on drafts of this book. I would also like to thank professionals from the education sector who have provided me with their valuable input. A special thank you goes to my wonderful family, Maria, Nya and Finny, who have kept me going with their support, laughter, fun and love. It has certainly been a very different kind of experience writing a book while being a new mum of twins! And finally, a massive thank you to Jessica Kingsley Publishers, as always!

Contents

About the Author

Hi! I'm Kate, and I have worked for several years providing support for children and young people on a range of emotional issues as well as training and guidance for parents and professionals. As a result, I have seen first-hand the extent of exam stress among young people today and the effects that it can have. So, writing a book on this topic was a must for me!

Starving the Exam Stress Gremlin is about empowering young people to feel confident when approaching exams and it provides ways in which the reader can ditch debilitating exam stress for good! I hope that you find within the pages of this book tips and tools that work for you, as well as stories from other young people to help and inspire you.

Happy reading and good luck with starving your Exam Stress Gremlin!

Kate

1

Why Read This Book?

If you have answered 'Yes' to any of these questions or if you are negatively affected by the pressure of exams and revision in other ways, then this workbook is here to help you!

Starving the Exam Stress Gremlin contains information and activities to help you understand what exam stress is, why it occurs and what you can do to get it under control. This isn't a 'study skills' or 'revision skills' book. It will provide some tips and strategies in these areas, but only those that will help you to reduce your exam stress. As that is what this workbook is all about – managing your exam stress!

Starving the Exam Stress Gremlin is based on something called cognitive behavioural therapy (CBT) and something called mindfulness. CBT is where a therapist helps people to deal with a wide range of emotional problems, including exam stress, by looking at the links between our:

COGNITION

The mental processes in our minds, such as thinking and remembering

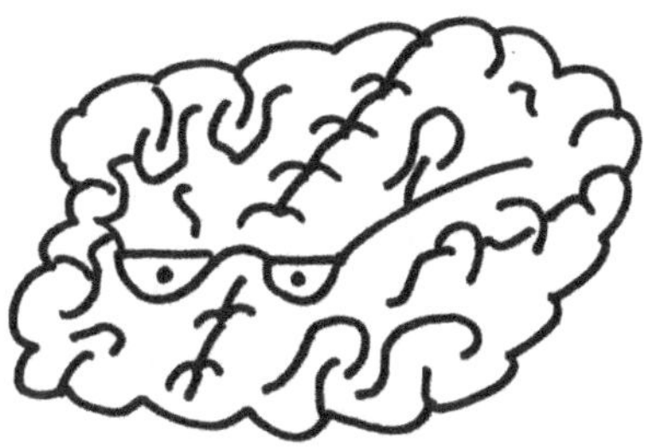

PHYSICAL REACTIONS

Things that happen in our bodies, such as feeling dizzy

EMOTIONS

Our feelings, such as scared or worried

BEHAVIOURS

How we act, such as avoiding situations

Mindfulness originates from the spiritual discipline of Buddhism and from meditation and yoga practices. When we practise mindfulness we make a choice to:

- become AWARE of our thoughts and feelings in the here and now
- ACCEPT our thoughts and feelings as they are without criticising or judging them or ourselves or viewing them as reality
- LET negative thoughts and feelings GO instead of focusing on them over and over again.

In the chapters and activities that follow, you will learn about how to apply CBT and mindfulness principles and techniques in order to starve your Exam Stress Gremlin and get your exam stress under control.

Many of the stress management strategies you will learn in this workbook can also be applied to other situations in which stress hinders you from performing or achieving as well as you could, such as performing in a school play or concert, attending a job interview, speaking in front of others or taking part in sporting competitions.

The way to get the most from *Starving the Exam Stress Gremlin* is to work through it in its entirety. But if you want to make a quick start, please feel free to just focus on the parts that are most relevant to you and your exam stress. And don't forget that you can always return to the other sections of the workbook in the future.

Also, it's important to remember that starting to explore your exam stress can sometimes raise difficult issues. If it does so for you, please consider talking to someone you trust about these issues, such as a parent, relative, friend, teacher or counsellor. Furthermore, for some young people, this workbook may not be the only help they will need. Sometimes, self-help tools alone are not sufficient to help a person make all the progress that they need to. In some cases, it is important to seek treatment from a mental health professional, such as a psychologist, psychiatrist, counsellor or therapist – for example, if a person's exam stress is accompanied by mental health disorders, such as depression or an eating disorder, or negative coping strategies like substance abuse or self-harming. If this is the case, this workbook is suitable to be used alongside professional support.

So now that you have learned about this workbook, its purpose, its basis and who it is suitable for, let's get started on starving your Exam Stress Gremlin and overcoming your exam stress!

2

What is Exam Stress and Who is the Exam Stress Gremlin?

Step one in managing exam stress is to understand what it actually is. In order to help you do this, I want us to travel back in time.

Destination – The Stone Age!

Your time machine jolts to a halt and you open the door. It is one million years ago and it's a time when cavemen and sabre-tooth tigers roam the Earth! Just in front of you is a caveman called Colin and behind him is a very vicious-looking creature preparing to pounce. Before you can shout 'It's behind you!' in true pantomime style, Caveman Colin turns and comes nose to nose with the sabre-tooth tiger!

Caveman Colin thinks...

When we have a thought, our bodies respond to what we are thinking. So earlier that morning when Caveman Colin was thinking about having breakfast, his stomach rumbled and his mouth watered, and whenever he thinks about his wife, Cavewoman Carol, and their Cave Kids, Crystal and Charlie, he smiles as his thoughts are happy.

But right now, Caveman Colin's thought about the threat of danger from the sabre-tooth tiger involves fear, and his body responds in a very different way! The fearful thought sets off a warning alarm in his body, just like smoke setting off a smoke alarm. And this warning alarm triggers the following temporary changes in his body that will help Caveman Colin to survive the very real danger he's in:

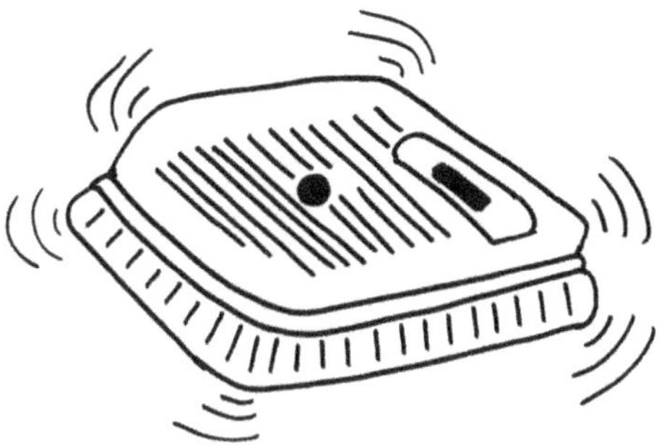

- Increased adrenalin, heart rate, pulse, blood pressure, breathing rate, pupil dilation, muscle tension, glucose energy and body temperature.
- Decreased digestive activity.
- Movement of blood to key muscles and the brain.

These changes in Caveman Colin's body will help him to:

RUN FASTER	THINK FASTER
SEE BETTER	BE STRONGER
HEAR BETTER	HEAL QUICKER

Altogether, these temporary changes in his body will help Caveman Colin to survive the meeting with the sabre-tooth tiger by:

DEFENDING HIMSELF

Or:

RUNNING AWAY TO SAFETY

This ancient survival mechanism is called the...

fight or flight response

...and it evolved to protect Caveman Colin, just like a suit of armour, from real dangers, such as an occasional encounter with a sabre-tooth tiger or even a woolly mammoth! Then once the danger was over, his fear would pass and the fight or flight response would stop.

Back to the Present Day

Let's get back into our time machines and fly forwards in time to the present day.

In today's world, sabre-tooth tigers and woolly mammoths are extinct and real dangers and emergencies are thankfully rare. But just like Caveman Colin, we still all get afraid sometimes in life. We can also get worried or nervous too at times. All these are normal feelings to have occasionally, such as feeling nervous just before an exam.

Today, when we are afraid, worried or nervous about something, we experience the same warning alarm and the same changes in our bodies that Caveman Colin did because we still all have a fight or flight response. This same reaction occurs whether the situation poses a real threat of danger or not as our bodies are responding to how we think about the situation, not the situation itself.

But this fight or flight response doesn't cause us any harm if we only experience it sometimes and if it calms down quickly – instead, it helps us to perform better or it protects us, just like it did for Caveman Colin!

But What If Your Warning Alarm Is Too Sensitive?

Unfortunately, some of us have frequent afraid, worried or nervous thoughts, often in situations that we see as threatening in some way even when there isn't a threat of real harm. This can make our warning alarm too sensitive and put us into an almost 'constant' state of fight or flight. This could be in response to thinking that lots of different types of situations in life are threatening, scary or too much to cope with in some way. Or we might just view one situation in life as too much to cope with, but because we think about it and worry about it so often, we still put ourselves in the constant fight or flight state.

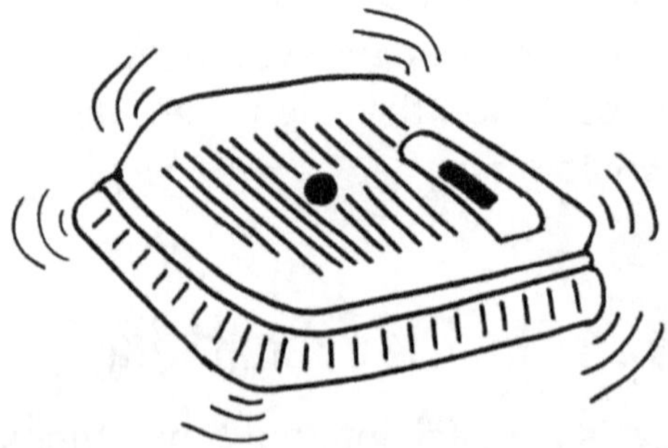

Exam Stress

When we are experiencing the fight or flight response too frequently because we think that the pressure and demands of exams are too much to cope with, we call this...

exam stress!

And research shows that exam stress is an increasing problem in today's society, especially as testing has become such a huge part of our culture with young people being exposed to messages about the importance of exam results for their futures and about how high grades equal success. This can lead many young people to wrongly believe that we are only worthy as individuals if we get good exam results and to discount the importance of enjoying learning and of other talents, skills and achievements in life, as Frankie's story on the next page shows.

FRANKIE'S WORLD

Frankie is 16 years old and is struggling to cope with the pressure of her upcoming exams. She is so worried that she won't be able to learn everything she needs to in time that she has stopped volunteering at a local hospital. Her teachers keep talking about the importance of getting good exam results and her parents are always telling other people about how proud they will be of her when she gets the place she wants at university. Frankie sees all of this as extra pressure.

Frankie believes she needs good grades to be a worthy person and feels useless as she doesn't think she is capable of achieving them. Frankie is so afraid of letting her parents and teachers down she cannot concentrate and nothing seems to stay in her memory. She is petrified that her mind will go blank in her exams and she will fail.

Frankie can't eat as she feels sick most of the time, and her heart races every time she thinks about exams. She spends every spare minute she has revising, but is just getting more and more exhausted. Frankie has forgotten about the importance of all her other achievements in life and the good things they show about her as a person, such as the kindness she shows in her voluntary work and all the skills and experience she has gained from it.

Unfortunately, our bodies weren't designed to be in a constant state of fight or flight. So when we suffer from exam stress, we frequently think, feel and act in ways that aren't good for us in response to revision and the upcoming exams, just like Frankie, resulting in a negative impact on us and our lives. For example, when we experience exam stress instead of just a few nerves, research shows that it can make it harder for us to revise and perform in our exams – just as it was for Frankie.

The Exam Stress Gremlin

And all of this makes a certain troublesome creature very happy. He's called the...

Exam Stress Gremlin!

The Exam Stress Gremlin wants you to be stressed – it's what gives him a meal, it's what makes him feel full! It's what makes him grow bigger and bigger and stronger and stronger! But don't despair if your Exam Stress Gremlin is currently huge – this workbook is here to help you starve him in order to get your exam stress under control!

In the Exam Stress Box on the next page or on your own piece of paper, draw a picture of your Exam Stress Gremlin and give him a name!

EXAM STRESS BOX

My Exam Stress Gremlin named ....

3

Our Stressed Minds

Why Some People Experience Exam Stress and Others Don't

Step two in managing exam stress is to understand how it develops. Why is it that some people experience high levels of exam stress and have huge Exam Stress Gremlins and others just experience occasional, normal pre-exam nerves? To help us answer this question, let's meet three young people facing an exam.

THREE FRIENDS AND A MATHS EXAM!

Three friends, Marley, Jason and Neela, aged 16, have their final maths exam coming up in a week's time. They each got a C grade in their last mock exam.

MARLEY

Every time Marley sits down to revise, he thinks, 'I can't do it. I'm useless. So what's the point?' As a result, he keeps putting the revision off and does anything he can to avoid it, even cleaning the house for his mum! By the end of the week, Marley has done very little studying and is starting to get very panicky at the thought of the exam. When he starts to panic, his heart races and he finds it hard to breathe. He ends up having to spend the entire night before the exam revising. ***Marley is experiencing exam stress!***

JASON

Jason finds it difficult to remember things for exams. He is constantly thinking, 'I will never be able to get it all to stay in my head in time for the exam. I will fail and my parents will think I'm stupid and hate me.' Jason feels so under pressure that he skips breakfast and lunch every day so that he can revise non-stop. His parents make him stop for dinner, but he eats very little as he has no appetite. He ends up having a row with either his mum or dad every night about not eating. By the end of the week, Jason has fallen out with all his family, including his two sisters, and feels bad about himself. He thinks, 'I am going to fail the exam because I'm a bad person and I don't deserve to pass,' and he has bad dreams the night before the exam. ***Jason is experiencing exam stress!***

NEELA

Neela knows that maths isn't her best subject at school but keeps thinking, 'If I revise hard and do the best I can, that is all that matters,' and, 'I can do it if I try.' She sets out a revision plan, sticks to it and takes regular breaks. She spends the evening before the exam listening to music to help her relax the few butterflies she has in her stomach and sleeps well that night. ***Neela is experiencing normal pre-exam nerves and is keeping calm.***

Q. Who or what is making Marley and Jason stressed? Tick your answer.

The exam and revision ☐ Their families ☐ Themselves ☐

A. When asked this question, a lot of people would say 'the exam and revision'. However, the answer is 'themselves'. Let's look at why.

Sources of stress, known as stressors, can be:

PEOPLE	PLACES
ACTIONS	THINGS
ATTITUDES	SITUATIONS

When we are experiencing exam stress, the stressors are exams and/or revision. We often believe that they are *making us* or *causing us* to be stressed – as though we have no control over whether we get stressed or not. This is what the Exam Stress Gremlin wants you to think! But if this was the case, then what would be the point in trying to control our exam stress? We would just be puppets on stressed-out strings!

And guess who'd be holding the puppet strings...your Exam Stress Gremlin!

But, thankfully, stressors *don't* make us do or feel anything. They are only ever...

triggers.

Think about it! If it was a situation that caused us stress, we would all feel and react in the same way in the same situation. But we don't, as the story about Marley, Jason and Neela shows.

Marley, Jason and Neela are all facing the same maths exam and they all got the same mark in their previous maths exam. And yet, Marley and Jason experience exam stress and Neela doesn't.

Q. Why do you think Marley and Jason are stressed but Neela isn't?

....

If you found it difficult to answer this question, take a look at each of their thoughts.

Neela is keeping calm because she...

thinks differently

...from Marley and Jason about the maths exam and her ability to cope with it.

Neela thinks realistically and positively, and as a result keeps calm and acts in constructive ways to help her get through it as best she can. However, Marley and Jason are thinking that the situation is worse than it actually is, that the exam is putting them under too much pressure and that they cannot cope. Marley and Jason are viewing exams through their...

Exam Stress Thinking Glasses!

What Are Exam Stress Thinking Glasses?

Here are some common types of Exam Stress Thinking Glasses:

MAGNIFYING GLASSES

When you think through these glasses everything seems bigger, worse, more important or more dangerous than it actually is!

For example, 'My life will be over if I don't pass these exams and my parents and friends will hate me.' *Debra-Jane, aged 10 years*

MAKE-BELIEVE GLASSES

When you think through these glasses you imagine things to be true even though you don't know whether they are true or not!

For example, 'I know I have done well in exams before, but I know these ones will be too hard. I'm definitely going to fail.' *Ben, aged 16 years*

FORTUNE-TELLING GLASSES

When you think through these glasses you predict that bad things will happen in the future! Your predictions often involve worst-case scenarios and failure!

For example, 'I'll freak out in my English exam, throw up and everyone will laugh at me.' *Jez, aged 15 years*

WHAT IF? GLASSES

When you think through these glasses you ask yourself, 'What if this bad thing happens?' or, 'What if that bad thing happens?' even though they are unlikely to happen!

For example, 'What if I don't pass my exams, and I disappoint my parents and they stop loving me?' *Mira, aged 16 years*

MIND-READING GLASSES

When you think through these glasses you imagine what other people are thinking – usually negative things about you – even though you don't actually know what people are thinking!

For example, 'I know my teachers think I'm too stupid to pass exams!' *Gavin, aged 11 years*

DOOM AND GLOOM GLASSES

When you think through these glasses you see the worst in everything around you, focus on the negatives and feel that everything is wrong or will go wrong!

For example, 'I always fail tests.' *Iona, aged 10 years*

I CAN'T GLASSES

When *you* think through these glasses *you* think *you* can't do things even though *you* can!

For example, 'My memory is useless, so I just can't pass tests.' *Candice, aged 10 years*

I'M USELESS GLASSES

When *you* think through these glasses *you* put *yourself* down and/or *compare yourself* negatively to others!

For example, 'I'm no good at anything, so what's the point in revising anyway?' *Theo, aged 11 years*

I SHOULD GLASSES

When *you* think through these glasses *you* think *you* should be perfect at things and not make mistakes. *You* also think that if *you're* not perfect, bad things will happen, that *you're* not good enough and that people won't like or love *you*!

For example, 'I should be able to get 100 per cent in my exams. If I can't, I'm useless.' *Rafiq, aged 15 years*

In the Exam Stress Box on the next page, write down the thoughts you frequently have about exams and revision and your ability to cope with them. Then write down which type of Exam Stress Thinking Glasses you are wearing for each thought.

EXAM STRESS BOX

THOUGHT	TYPE OF EXAM STRESS THINKING GLASSES

Exam stress thinking

Because it is how we...

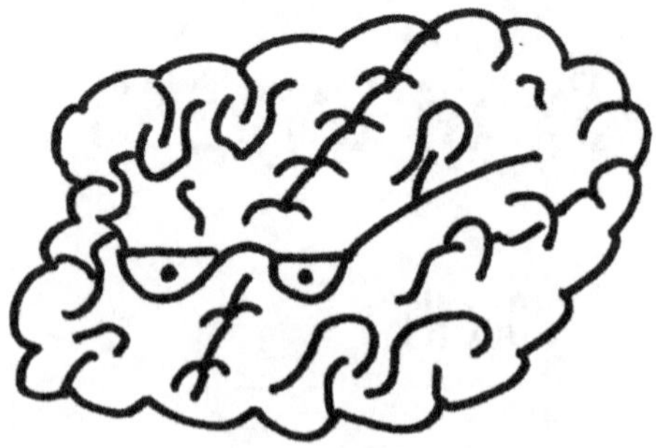

think

...about a situation that leads to a stressful reaction towards it, the Exam Stress Gremlin wants us to wear our Exam Stress Thinking Glasses all the time, like Marley and Jason. He wants us to think that revision and exams are worse than they actually are. He wants us to blow them out of proportion. He wants us to think that our whole life's happiness and survival depend on the results we get in an exam and that if we do badly it will be the end of the world. He wants us to think that there is no way to cope and that if we can't cope then we are failures. Why?

Because the Exam Stress Gremlin wants us to be stressed. He wants us to fall apart under the pressure! Remember, it's what gives him a meal!

So, the more we think in negative and unrealistic ways about exams and revision and our ability to cope with them using our Exam Stress Thinking Glasses, the more we...

feed our Exam Stress Gremlin

...making him bigger and bigger and fuller and fuller and us more and more stressed!

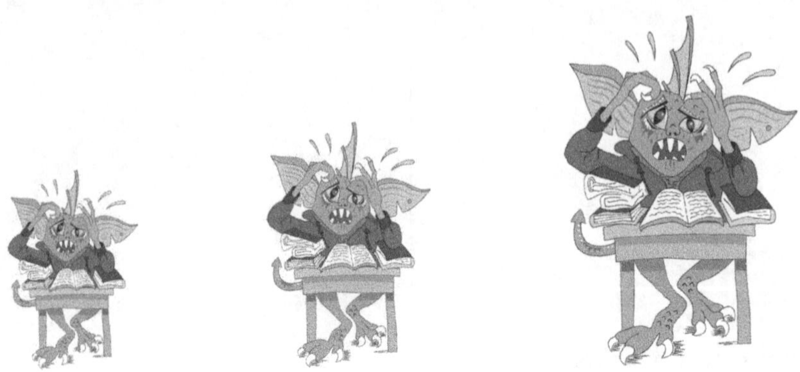

And the more stressed we get, the harder and harder it is to take our Exam Stress Thinking Glasses off and stressed-out thoughts get stuck in our heads.

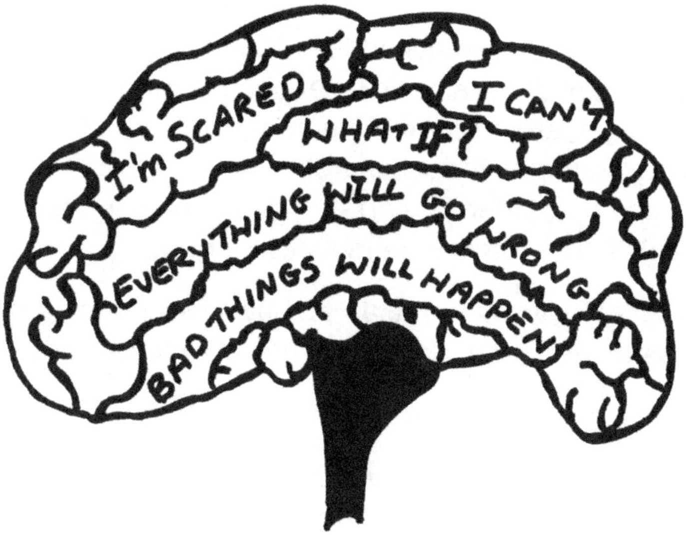

They play over and over again in our minds, just like a song on repeat on our mobile phones!

And just like it did for Marley and Jason, this constant negative and unrealistic thinking leads to us feeling bad physically and emotionally and acting in ways that hinder us further, as you will see in the next chapter.

It can be especially hard not to think in these negative and unrealistic ways about exams and revision as we are often exposed to messages from those around us about the importance of exams. These messages are often well meaning, but it can be hard not to see them as adding to the pressure!

It can also be harder for certain people to keep their thoughts about exams and revision in perspective if they:

- are already going through or have been through ***difficult, stressful, distressing or traumatic life experiences***
- have experienced ***exams that haven't gone well*** in the past
- are experiencing ***negative comments about themselves and their abilities from other people*** around them, such as family, peers or teachers
- are experiencing ***unrealistic expectations from others***, such as parents or teachers
- have been ***exposed to other people responding to life situations in stressful ways***
- are experiencing or have experienced ***other emotional or mental health issues***, such as depression or anxiety
- have ***a disability that can hinder learning***.

These all have the potential to make us more susceptible to:

- thinking, feeling and acting in negative ways
- feeding our Exam Stress Gremlins
- experiencing exam stress.

However, they do not *cause* us to have exam stress, they just make us ***more susceptible*** to experiencing it. But we don't have to be like this. We have a choice as to how we respond to exam- and revision-related situations, as you will learn later in this workbook.

So, don't be disheartened if what you have read so far reminds you of you, as this workbook will teach you more about exam stress and tips and strategies to help you to starve your Exam Stress Gremlin and get rid of exam stress for good!

4

Our Stressed Bodies, Emotions and Behaviours

What Keeps Exam Stress Going?

Step three in managing our exam stress is to understand what keeps exam stress going. Let's look at this using something called the Exam Stress Gremlin Cycle.

The Exam Stress Gremlin Cycle

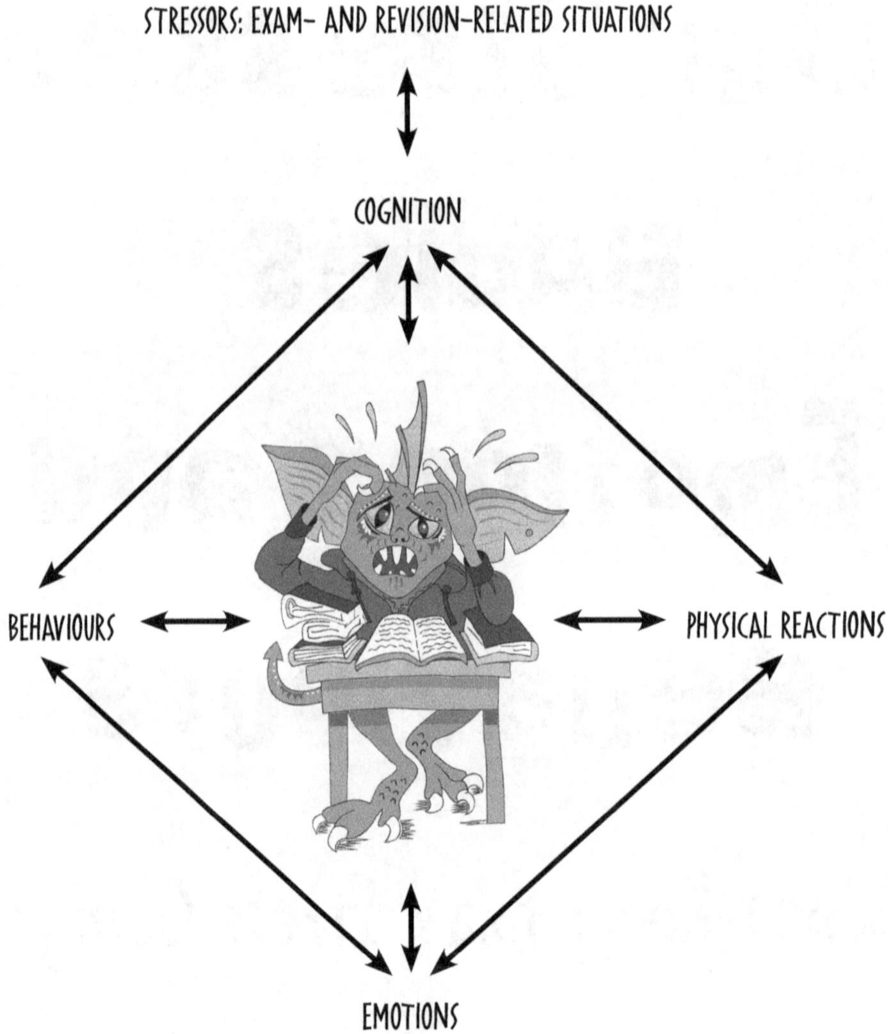

The Exam Stress Gremlin Cycle is based on a cognitive behavioural approach. It highlights how exam stress is maintained due to an interaction between the stressors of exams and revision and our:

COGNITION

The mental processes in our minds, such as thinking and remembering

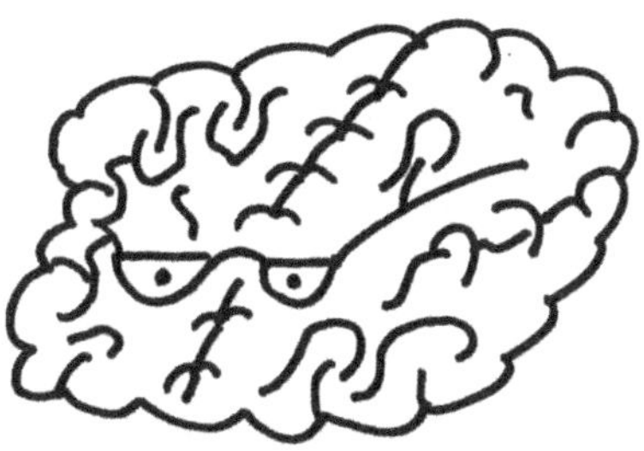

PHYSICAL REACTIONS

Things that happen in our bodies, such as feeling dizzy

EMOTIONS

Our feelings, such as scared or worried

BEHAVIOURS

How we act, such as avoiding situations

The cycle shows that it is how we...

think about exams and revision and our ability to cope with them

...that affects:

- our brain's ability to function in other ways, such as remembering things
- how our bodies react physically
- how we feel emotionally
- and how we then choose to behave.

So, let's look at each part of the Exam Stress Gremlin Cycle with the help of an 11-year-old-girl called Sadie who has exams in three weeks' time.

Exam Stress Cognition

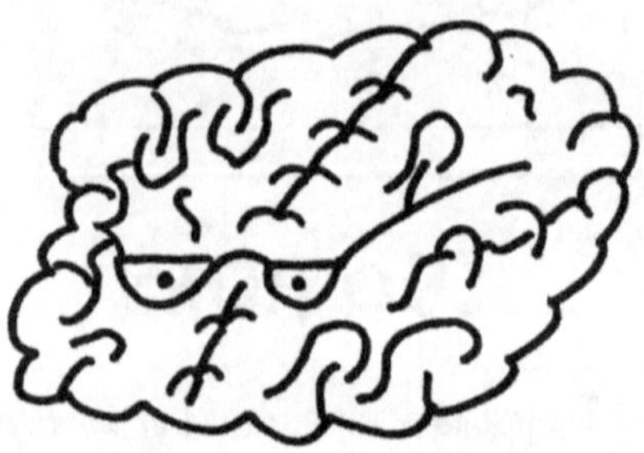

The first part of the Exam Stress Gremlin Cycle recaps what we learned in the previous chapter, namely that:

- if we think about exams and revision (the stressors) negatively and unrealistically using our Exam Stress Thinking Glasses, we feed our Exam Stress Gremlin and experience exam stress
- the more we feed our Exam Stress Gremlin, the more likely we are to think negatively and unrealistically about our ability to cope with exams and revision as well – thus feeding our Exam Stress Gremlin some more!

- the more we think negatively and unrealistically, the more we feed our Exam Stress Gremlin, the bigger and bigger he gets and the more stressed we are likely to be!

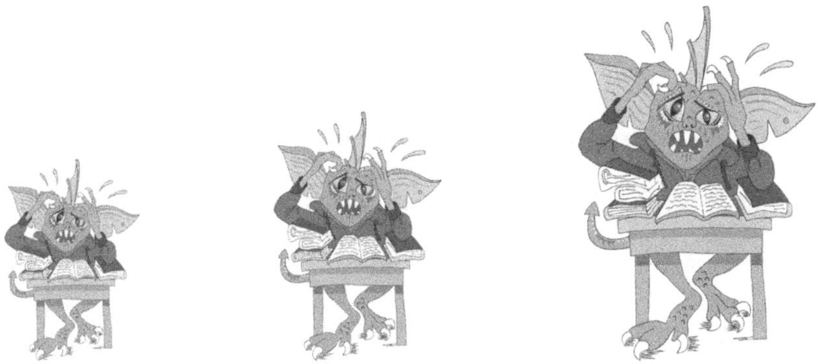

Sadie's thoughts about her upcoming exams are a good example of feeding an Exam Stress Gremlin by thinking negatively and unrealistically, as you will see from the picture below.

When we frequently think negatively and unrealistically about exams, we can experience other cognitive symptoms as well. For example, we can feel as if our minds have 'gone blank' and we can find it hard to:

- concentrate, focus and pay attention
- retrieve information from our memory
- understand information (what we call 'comprehension')
- follow processes or sequences
- gather our thoughts into a logical and clear format
- put our thoughts down on paper or say them out loud in a reasoned and clear way.

All of these can make it hard for us to learn information, store it into our memories and then recall it in exam situations.

Experiencing these other cognitive symptoms worsens our thoughts about exams and our ability to succeed at them and our Exam Stress Gremlins get even bigger and our stress levels increase further!

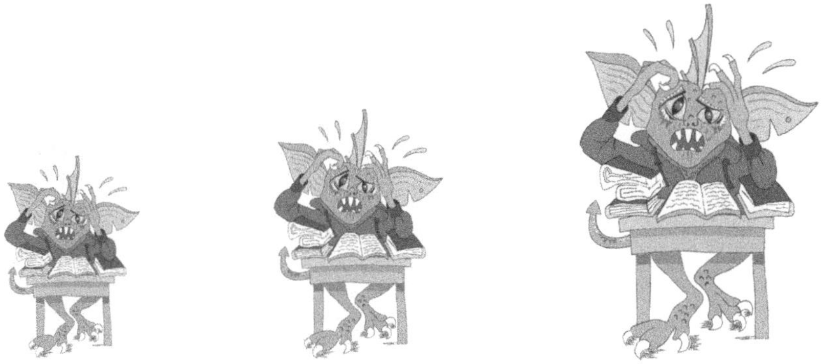

Exam Stress Physical Reactions

The Exam Stress Gremlin Cycle also shows that when we frequently think negatively and unrealistically about exams and revision and our ability to cope with them, we can trigger negative physical reactions in our bodies, such as dizziness.

Sadie's physical reactions include headaches, stomach aches, loss of appetite and feeling sick all the time.

The more we experience negative physical reactions like Sadie, the more we feed our Exam Stress Gremlin, the bigger and bigger he gets and the more and more stressed we become.

In the Exam Stress Box on the next page are a range of negative physical reactions that we can experience when we are stressed. Highlight or colour in any that apply to you when you are feeling stressed in response to exams and revision.

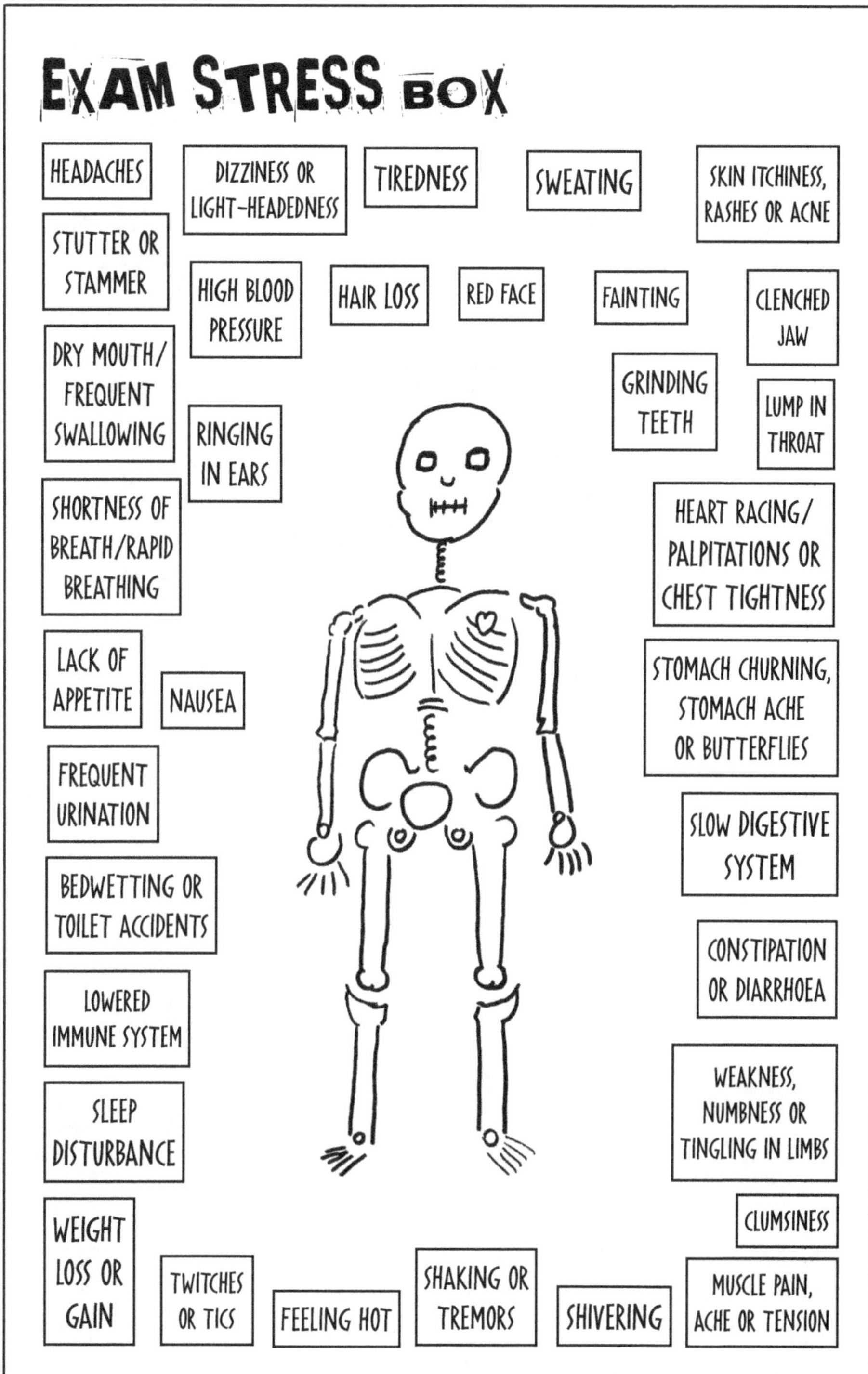

Exam stress physical reactions

Exam Stress Emotions

The Exam Stress Gremlin Cycle also shows that when we frequently think negatively and unrealistically about exams and revision and our ability to cope with them, we can trigger off negative emotions as part of exam stress.

For Sadie, this involves feeling:

- A sense of dread
- Panicky
- Worthless
- Afraid
- Tense
- Hopeless
- Overwhelmed
- Ashamed
- Worried

The more we experience these other negative emotions, the more we feed our Exam Stress Gremlin, the bigger he gets and the more stressed we become.

In the Exam Stress Box on the next page are a range of negative emotions that we can experience as part of exam stress. Highlight or colour in any that apply to you when you are feeling stressed in response to exams and revision.

EXAM STRESS BOX

UPSET
PARANOIA
AGITATION
RESTLESSNESS
ENVY
WORRY
FRUSTRATION
PANIC
LOW IN CONFIDENCE
FEELING INADEQUATE OR INFERIOR
FEELING OVERWHELMED
LOW MOOD
IRRITABILITY
NERVOUSNESS
LACK OF RESILIENCE
HYPERSENSITIVITY
LONELINESS
CONFUSION
HOPELESSNESS
DREAD
DISAPPOINTMENT
SADNESS
DISTRESS
INSECURITY
ANXIETY
DEFENSIVENESS
EDGINESS/ EASILY STARTLED
FEELING UNDER PRESSURE
FEELING WORTHLESS
FEELING OUT OF CONTROL
SELF-BLAME
SELF-DOUBT
SELF-LOATHING
NUMBNESS
TENSION
SHAME
HELPLESSNESS
FEELING TRAPPED OR CLAUSTROPHOBIC
LOSS OF SENSE OF HUMOUR
LOSS OF MOTIVATION, PLEASURE OR INTEREST
FEAR
ANGER
UNHAPPINESS
HUMILIATION

Exam stress emotions

Exam Stress Behaviours

Finally, the Exam Stress Gremlin Cycle shows that the more we think in negative and unrealistic ways and experience negative physical reactions and emotions, the more likely it is that we will start acting in ways that aren't good for us, such as avoiding situations, which feeds our Exam Stress Gremlin further, making him bigger and bigger and us more and more stressed!

In the Exam Stress Box on the following pages is a list of ways in which people can act when they are experiencing exam stress. Tick any that you do regularly because of exam stress.

EXAM STRESS BOX

BEHAVIOUR	APPLIES TO ME
Avoid or put off doing revision or revision planning or parts of revision, such as subjects you find harder	
Waste time doing other things instead of the revision you should be doing	
Quit/give up part way through doing revision or don't stick to revision plan	
Give up on revising before you've even tried	
Avoid going to school	
Avoid certain lessons at school	
Avoid revision sessions at school	
Leave school or specific lessons early or arrive late for school or specific lessons	
Avoid an exam	
Quit part way through an exam	
Avoid other exam- or revision-related situations, such as talking to people about exams or school	
Planning escape routes out of exam- or revision-related situations	

BEHAVIOUR	APPLIES TO ME
Stop doing fun things	
Avoid making decisions	
Avoid leaving your bed, bedroom or the house	
Sleep more or less than usual	
Hide away from people, such as stop going out with or playing with friends	
Neglect personal appearance or physical hygiene	
Hide how you are feeling from other people	
Study/revise excessively	
Act in ways to please other people	
Act angrily towards yourself	
Act aggressively or irritably towards others	
Argue with others	
Take your feelings out on others	
Break off a relationship or friendship	
Act in defensive ways	
Act in defiant or non-compliant ways	

BEHAVIOUR	APPLIES TO ME
Act in disruptive ways	
Put yourself down or criticise yourself when you speak	
Cry	
Skip meals	
Binge eat or comfort eat	
Make yourself sick after eating	
Exercise excessively	
Drink or take drugs	
Bottle your stress up inside you	
Do things that get you into trouble or commit risk-taking behaviours, such as stealing or truancy	
Self-harm	
Follow rituals or routines obsessively or act in compulsive ways, such as checking things that don't need to be checked	
Act in ways to get other people's attention	
Seek reassurance from others about exams and your ability to do well	

BEHAVIOUR	APPLIES TO ME
Stay close to a certain person or people as much as possible, such as not wanting to be apart from your mum	
Need items as a comfort, such as a favourite soft toy or a 'lucky charm'	
Act in restless ways, such as pacing, fidgeting or have difficulties sitting still	
Talk more or less quickly	
Ignore the advice of others	
Get easily distracted	

Exam stress behaviours

We often act in the ways listed in the Exam Stress Box above because we think they will bring short-term benefits. For example, you may put off or avoid doing revision as you think it is better to have not tried than to have tried your best and not done as well as you would have liked. However, these behaviours actually have negative impacts on us in both the short and long term, and, as a result, we call them...

self-defeating behaviours.

For example, Sadie revises every evening, weekend and all through the night when she should be asleep as she is so afraid of forgetting what she has learned and disappointing her family. As a result, she

is tired and burnt out. She also doesn't eat as she doesn't feel hungry, so her energy levels are low, and she cries whenever anyone mentions the exams at school, which is making her feel more and more worthless and ashamed.

The more self-defeating our behaviours become, the more we feed our Exam Stress Gremlin and the more stressed we become.

Plus:

- the worse we feel physically and emotionally
- the harder we find it to perform the mental processes needed to revise and complete exams, such as concentrating and remembering
- the more negative and unrealistic thoughts we have about exams and our ability to cope with them.

In addition, self-defeating behaviours prevent us from:

- seeing that the bad things we worry about happening are unlikely to happen and that even if they did we would cope with them
- finding out how differently we could think and feel about our abilities and exams if we didn't behave in these ways
- finding out that the assumptions we make are not realistic or accurate
- discovering more constructive and positive ways to cope with exam stress.

The result – we end up stuck in the middle of a very vicious cycle of exam stress, where we keep focusing on the fact we are stressed and not on how to deal with exams and revision in a constructive way. And it is this never-ending cycle of negative cognition, physical reactions, emotions and behaviours that keeps exam stress going by feeding your Exam Stress Gremlin – enabling him to get bigger and bigger and your exam stress worse and worse!

This can lead to a whole host of other negative impacts on us and our lives, as we will see in the next chapter.

5

Impacts of Exam Stress

The fourth step in managing your exam stress and starving your Exam Stress Gremlin is to understand the different types of negative impacts that experiencing exam stress can have. Think about your experience of exam stress and write down in the Exam Stress Box below the negative impacts you think it has had on you and your life.

EXAM STRESS BOX

Impacts of exam stress on me and my life

You may have talked about the impacts your exam stress has had on your:

- physical health
- mental health and emotional well-being
- relationships
- social and leisure activities
- academic achievements
- goals for the future.

PHYSICAL HEALTH

Impacts on our physical health can include:

- experiencing exhaustion or burn out due to working too hard
- becoming more susceptible to illness, such as digestive disorders or migraines, or making current illnesses, allergies or pain levels worse due to the level of stress or working too hard
- experiencing negative physical effects as a result of behaviours that aren't good for us health wise, such as severe weight loss and a lack of energy from undereating
- and experiencing the other physical reactions in our bodies that we discussed in Chapter 4.

MENTAL HEALTH AND EMOTIONAL WELL-BEING

Impacts on our mental health and emotional well-being can include:

- developing other emotional and mental health conditions alongside stress, such as depression, anxiety, obsessive compulsive disorder (OCD), phobias, addictions and eating disorders
- experiencing any of the other negative emotions that we discussed in Chapter 4
- developing low self-esteem, lowered self-belief and less confidence in our ability to cope with exams in the future and in other areas of our lives
- judging our worth based on exam results
- using negative coping strategies, such as self-harming and substance misuse
- feeling as if life is not worth living and having suicidal thoughts
- lower happiness and life satisfaction levels.

RELATIONSHIPS

Various stresses, strains and pressures can occur in our relationships with family, friends, boyfriends and girlfriends, teachers and other important people in our lives if, as a result of exam stress, we:

- withdraw from interacting socially with others
- seek constant reassurance or attention from others
- take our emotions out on others
- act in negative ways towards others, such as being aggressive
- focus so much on our own negative thoughts and feelings that we ignore or neglect the needs and feelings of others
- have a lack of confidence and self-belief
- have a belief that we will disappoint others or they will no longer like us or love us if we don't meet what we believe to be their high expectations of us
- have negative beliefs about ourselves.

These factors can make it harder for us to maintain existing relationships and also to start new ones, and can lead us to feel isolated from others socially. People close to us can also be worried about us because of our exam stress, which can also impact on those relationships.

SOCIAL AND LEISURE ACTIVITIES

Exam stress can prevent us from living life to the full as we will often:

- not want to be around other people
- waste time stressing and worrying that could have been spent on more fun activities
- avoid enjoyable and social activities due to the way our stress makes us feel
- feel less interested in or motivated to do fun things!

Alternatively, we may work excessively due to fear of failure, leaving no time for enjoyable activities.

ACADEMIC ACHIEVEMENTS

Exam stress can hinder our performance academically because it can involve:

- memory and concentration difficulties
- problems reading and interpreting questions
- a lack of belief in our abilities
- avoiding or putting off studying and revising
- avoiding or escaping from lessons or exams
- wasting time stressing and worrying instead of studying and revising.

All of these can disrupt our learning and memory recall, and lead us to make more mistakes, which in turn hinder our ability to demonstrate our true knowledge and skills in exams.

GOALS FOR THE FUTURE

Exam stress and all its various symptoms and effects can combine to have a major impact on our:

- motivation to achieve our future goals and desires
- belief in our ability to achieve them
- actual ability to achieve them.

It can also lead us to have very few goals and desires in the first place.

All these negative impacts feed our Exam Stress Gremlin further, making him bigger and bigger and keeping us stuck in that vicious cycle of exam stress. But, please don't be disheartened by this! It is possible to break out of this vicious cycle and get rid of your Exam Stress Gremlin for good, as the rest of this workbook will show!

6

You're Not On Your Own in Experiencing Exam Stress

Step five in managing your exam stress and starving the Exam Stress Gremlin is realising you are not on your own in experiencing exam stress. Researchers have asked children and young people about exam stress through face-to-face interviews and online and paper surveys. I can't show you every piece of research that has been conducted as that would take too much time away from your revision! But the examples that you will read about in the following Exam Stress Journal clearly highlight that you are not on your own, as exam stress affects many children and young people today.

The Exam Stress Journal

Exam Stress Affects Many

Exam stress has the potential to affect young people of all backgrounds, with research showing that children as young as seven years old are worrying about exams (Connor 2003; Putwain 2008). And it is clear that many children and young people today are affected. For example:

- A Scout Association survey of 13-18-year-olds found that 90 per cent felt under pressure to achieve high grades at school and in exams (Scout Association 2007).
- A recent ChildLine National Exam Stress Survey (NSPCC 2015b) found that 96 per cent felt anxious about exams and revision.
- A Girl Guides Association (2008) survey found that 74 per cent felt worried about exams and tests.
- A survey of 1000 pupils aged 10-11 years old who had recently taken exams in the UK found that 68 per cent had felt pressured at the time of the exams (Kellogg's 2015).
- A 2015 UK study for the National Union of Teachers (Hutchings 2015) found that 90 per cent of the teachers surveyed reported pupils becoming very stressed and anxious prior to exams.

The Exam Stress Journal Page 1

Exam Stress on the Rise

It is also clear that exam stress levels are increasing. For example, in 2013/14, 58 per cent of counselling sessions conducted by ChildLine in relation to school and education problems were about exam stress – a 200 per cent rise on the previous year. The NSPCC also reported that there were more than 87,500 visits to the ChildLine website over the same issue that year (NSPCC 2014).

The number of counselling sessions conducted about exam stress had increased by a further 9 per cent to a total of 3077 sessions by 2014/15 (NSPCC 2015a) and by a further 11 per cent to 4204 in 2015/16 (NSPCC 2016).

Sources of Pressure

What Will People Think?

Research shows that young people experiencing exam stress are commonly afraid of failure (NSPCC 2015a); letting down or disappointing others, such as their parents and teachers (NSPCC 2015a and 2016); and of being judged negatively by others (Young Researchers Dorset 2014). For example, some young people contacting ChildLine were worried about their peers thinking they were 'stupid' if they didn't do well in an exam (NSPCC 2014), others reported struggling under the pressure of trying to achieve high grades to

meet their parents' expectations (NSPCC 2014, 2015a and 2016), and others were worried about what people would think of them if they needed to ask teachers or parents for help (NSPCC 2016).

The Exam Stress Journal Page 2

What If I Ruin My Future?

Some young people report feeling stressed and under pressure as they believe that their exam results will determine their future life outcomes and choices (Young Researchers Dorset 2014), such as what sets they are put in at secondary school, whether they will be bullied over their results, whether their results will stop them making friends and whether their results will stop them achieving their future ambitions (NSPCC 2014). As a result, research shows that recognised public examinations (for example, SATS and GCSEs in the UK) lead to higher levels of exam stress than everyday classroom tests (for example, Putwain 2008). And teachers emphasising the importance of exams and consequences of exam failure for students only make the pressure worse for many according to recent research (for example, Putwain and Best 2011 and 2012).

It's All Too Much!

In 2015/16, young people attending ChildLine counselling sessions for exam stress stated that the exam process overwhelmed them and that excessive workloads, struggling with subjects and not being prepared for exams contributed to their stress and anxiety (NSPCC 2016). Other young people reported a lack of support in dealing with exams as also exacerbating their stress (NSPCC 2015b and 2016).

The Exam Stress Journal Page 3

The Signs and Symptoms of Exam Stress

The most frequently reported signs and symptoms of exam stress by young people accessing ChildLine counselling sessions in 2015/16 were feeling low, panic attacks, excessive crying, low self-esteem, self-harming and suicidal thoughts (NSPCC 2016). Eating disorders and arguments with parents were also reported in 2013/14 (NSPCC 2014).

The ChildLine National Exam Stress Survey (NSPCC 2015b) found that almost half of those surveyed were skipping meals, and 14 per cent were using drugs and alcohol as coping mechanisms. In a 2013 YouGov online poll of 2342 young people aged 16-25, 20 per cent stated that their worry about exams was affecting their health and 17 per cent reported having panic attacks (The Prince's Trust 2013). And a 2008 survey by the Girl Guides Association found that almost a fifth of those surveyed felt bad about themselves as a result of exams.

A study for the National Union of Teachers in the UK (Hutchings 2015) reported students self-harming, missing school, and having panic attacks, depression, eating disorders,

perfectionist beliefs, low confidence and low motivation. One teacher talked about 10- and 11-year-olds in 'complete meltdown'.

Sleep disturbance is also a commonly reported symptom of exam stress. The ChildLine National Exam Stress Survey (NSPCC 2015b) found that two-thirds of young people were having difficulties sleeping; 15 per cent of those surveyed in the YouGov poll for The Prince's Trust (2013) were unable to sleep at night because of the worry of exams; and sleepless nights

The Exam Stress Journal Page 4

and fear before tests were also reported by many of those surveyed for the Girl Guides Association (2008). Similarly, interviews conducted with students aged 16-18 from three schools in Dorset in 2014 (Young Researchers Dorset 2014) found that the most commonly reported exam stress symptoms were sleep problems and associated tiredness. Twenty-two per cent of 1000 UK 10- and 11-year-olds surveyed in 2015 who had recently taken exams had lost sleep as a result (Kellogg's 2015).

Impacts of Exam Stress

Research shows that the symptoms of exam stress can have a negative impact on exam performance. For example, some students report feeling a failure prior to their exams and they therefore have no motivation to revise or study as it is seen as pointless (NSPCC 2016).

Others find that their anxious thoughts take over their brains, making it difficult to concentrate during revision and to read, understand and remember what they revise. The same applies to concentrating, memory recall and understanding exam questions during the exams themselves. For example, interviews conducted with students aged 16-18 in Dorset (Young Researchers Dorset 2014) found that the most commonly reported negative effects on academic achievement included problems with concentrating and a decreased ability to revise.

All of these negative impacts make it harder to get the exam results we are truly capable of.

The Exam Stress Journal Page 5

YOUR VOICE! (PART 1)

If you could have your say on what is needed to address exam stress issues in young people today, what would you tell the politicians? Write a letter to your government with your suggestions in the space below. You can produce a copy of this letter and send it to your local politician. Also, why not sign up to the Young Minds school stress campaign #FightThePressure at www.youngmindsvs.org.uk?

Tell the government what you think!

Now take a look at the following pictures, poems and songs by other young people where they describe what exam stress is like for them.

My Exam Stress Rap

Exam stress,
Has made my life a mess.
I will never pass a memory test.
My results will only ever depress.
I know I will never impress.
Thanks to me, my mum will just feel disappointment and distress.
My uselessness is impossible to suppress,
And I will never know success.
So as I said...exam stress,
Has made my life a mess!

By Frankie, aged 15 years

By Michael, aged 11 years

Revision – What's the Point?

My exams are in a few weeks.
But I can't sleep, I can't eat.
I feel like such a weak freak!

I sit in front of my revision books,
But I'm too scared to even take a look.

I can't stop thoughts of failure whizzing through my head.
All I want to do is hide under the covers of my bed.

I know I'll just disappoint my parents, so what's the point in trying?
Instead I'll just sit here and keep on crying.

'Work hard, do well and you'll get a great job' is all that I hear.
My results being rubbish, and my life being
over, is therefore what I fear.

I wish I could cope?
I wish I could be strong?
Instead I've given up hope,
As all I'll do is get the answers wrong.

By Neave, aged 16 years

By Tamara, aged 11 years

I Can't Think, I'm Going to Sink, I Feel on the Brink

I can't think
I'm going to sink
I feel on the brink.

I can't think
My brain is mush
I feel on the brink.

I can't think
I'm on edge
I feel on the brink.

I can't think
My hands shake
I feel on the brink.

I can't think
I can't breathe
I feel on the brink.

I can't think
Of anything positive
I feel on the brink.

I can't think
I can't concentrate
I feel on the brink.

I can't think
I can't remember
I feel on the brink.

I can't think
I can't revise
I feel on the brink.

I can't think
I can't achieve
I feel on the brink.

I can't think
I can't succeed
I feel on the brink.

I can't think
I can't stop crying
I feel on the brink.

I can't think
I hate myself
I feel on the brink.

I can't think
I will never pass
I feel on the brink.

I can't think
I'm going to sink
I feel on the brink...
of hopelessness,
failure and despair.

By Orla, aged 15 years

I'm So Worried

I'm so worried
That I will forget all that I've learnt

I'm so worried
That I will get things wrong

I'm so worried
That I will do rubbish

I'm so worried
That my mind will go blank

I'm so worried
That I'll look stupid

I'm so worried
That my mum and dad will be upset

I'm so worried
I'm so worried
I'm so worried

By Henry, aged 10 years

By Gabriel, aged 15 years

In the following Exam Stress Box, try showing what your exam stress is like through one of the following creative methods – but only if it won't put extra pressure on you right now:

- Draw a picture or take a photo or series of photos.
- Write a song, rap or poem.
- Write a short story or play.
- Write a blog.
- Draw or write down ideas for a short film.
- Draw or write down ideas for a dance piece.

EXAM STRESS BOX

Let's get creative

7

Starving the Exam Stress Gremlin

Thinking Differently!

The sixth and seventh steps in managing your exam stress and starving your Exam Stress Gremlin are...

THINK DIFFERENTLY	and	ACT DIFFERENTLY

Do you remember that it is how you think about exams and revision that causes your exam stress? Do you remember that if you are wearing your Exam Stress Thinking Glasses you are feeding your Exam Stress Gremlin? To stop this and to starve your Exam Stress Gremlin, you need to learn how to...

think differently!

And that is what this chapter is all about! (Acting differently is covered in Chapter 8.) The three methods of thinking differently that we are going to look at are:

- accepting that thoughts are only thoughts
- ditching your Exam Stress Thinking Glasses
- visualisation.

So, let's start with the first way in which you can think differently.

Accepting that Thoughts Are Only Thoughts

In Chapter 1 of this workbook I told you a little bit about something called mindfulness. Mindfulness can help us to starve our Exam Stress Gremlins by teaching us to:

- become AWARE of our thoughts in the here and now
- ACCEPT our thoughts are only thoughts and that they can't hurt us unless we let them

- LET our thoughts GO, just like leaves blowing away in the wind.

Let's have a go at an exercise to help you practice letting go of your thoughts. Get a piece of paper and write a negative thought that you have about your exams on it. Then say out loud, 'This is only a thought and it cannot hurt me.' Next, screw up the piece of paper and throw it into a bin, and as you do, imagine your thought blowing away in the wind, just like those leaves! And visualise your Exam Stress Gremlin shrinking!

Let's now look at another way of thinking differently.

Ditching Your Exam Stress Thinking Glasses

Earlier in this workbook we learned about different types of Exam Stress Thinking Glasses. And remember, the more we wear our Exam Stress Thinking Glasses by thinking in negative and unrealistic ways about exams, the more we feed our Exam Stress Gremlin and the more stressed we get. So how do we ditch our Exam Stress Thinking Glasses and starve our Exam Stress Gremlin? By challenging our negative and unrealistic thoughts using something called...

realistic thinking.

Realistic thinking involves searching for facts, just like a detective searching for evidence. To search for facts, ask yourself questions like those on the next page.

What am I thinking?

Is this thought helpful right now?

What are the facts about the situation?

Is my thought based on the facts?

Do I have any evidence to back up my thought?

What are the advantages and disadvantages of my thought?

Am I thinking factually about the present or am I imagining the future or obsessing over the past?

Which pair of Exam Stress Thinking Glasses am I wearing?

What will the effects of this way of thinking be on my body, emotions and behaviours?

What is the worst thing that could happen and is it really that likely?

If the worst thing happened, would it really be that bad or would I cope somehow?

What is more likely to happen?

What would I tell a friend in the same situation?

What is a more realistic way of thinking about the situation based on the facts?

What will be the effects of thinking a more realistic thought?

The more you think differently by searching for the facts, the following should happen:

- You should be wearing your Exam Stress Thinking Glasses less and less.
- You should be starving your Exam Stress Gremlin.
- You should be feeling less and less stressed.

And your Exam Stress Gremlin should shrink more and more!

So, whenever you find yourself putting on your Exam Stress Thinking Glasses, take them off and start to think more realistically about your exams, revision and your ability to cope with them based on the facts. Make sure you aren't being overly negative in some way or blowing things out of proportion. Remember, situations are normally not as bad as we think they are going to be, and even if our worst-case scenario actually occurs, we can find a way to cope with it, learn from it and move on from it.

This isn't easy to do and can take some practice, but it is well worth trying! Some people find thinking of a red traffic light or a stop sign when they have a negative or unrealistic thought helps them to break out of that thought ready to challenge it. This is called 'thought stopping'.

Let's look at an example to give you some practice at thinking realistically.

MATILDA'S STORY

Matilda is 16 years old. She is revising hard for her final secondary school exams, but she is struggling with Geography. She is getting more and more upset by this and is now finding it difficult to concentrate on any of her revision. She can't stop thinking, 'I'm going to fail my Geography exams, and if I do my mum and dad will think I'm stupid.' She also spends a lot of time thinking, 'I'm a useless person, I should be perfect at everything, and if I'm no good at Geography, then I'm going to do rubbish in the rest of my exams as well,' even though she always does well in her other subjects. She wakes up at night thinking, 'I'll go into complete meltdown in my exams, everyone will laugh and my life will be over. I'll never make anything of myself because of failing my exams.'

Q. Are Matilda's thoughts based on facts? Tick your answer.

a) Yes ☐ b) No ☐

Q. Is Matilda wearing Exam Stress Thinking Glasses? Tick your answer.

a) Yes ☐ b) No ☐

Q. If your answer was 'Yes', which ones do you think she is wearing?

....

....

....

Q. Which are the thoughts that Matilda could accept as only thoughts and let go of or challenge based on facts?

....

....

....

Q. What realistic thoughts could Matilda have instead?

....

....

....

If you said that Matilda's thoughts aren't based on facts, you are correct. Matilda is wearing a number of different types of Exam Stress Thinking Glasses, such as:

- magnifying glasses
- make-believe glasses
- fortune-telling glasses
- mind-reading glasses
- I'm useless glasses
- I should glasses.

Matilda needs to let go of her negative thoughts about herself and her exams and think more realistically. She needs to realise that struggling with one subject does not make her stupid, that no one is perfect, and that she has lots of evidence that she is good at her other subjects.

Some people find it easier to challenge their thoughts by saying them out loud or to other people. Others find writing the process down more helpful, especially in the initial stages. This allows you to use these notes again in the future if you have similar thoughts. The Alternative Thoughts Worksheet that follows will help you with this. It will help you to start ditching your Exam Stress Thinking Glasses, think more realistically and starve your Exam Stress Gremlin!

Alternative Thoughts Worksheet

Write your answers to the questions in the spaces below.

What is the exam- or revision-related stressor?

What am I thinking?

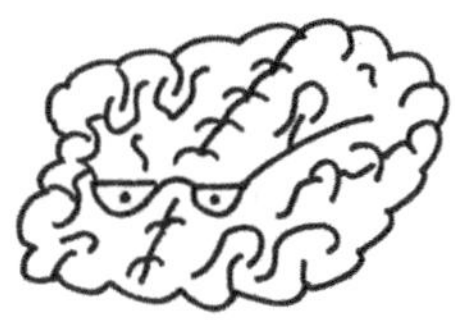

Am I thinking through any of the following Exam Stress Thinking Glasses? (Colour in any that apply to your thoughts.)

MAGNIFYING GLASSES	WHAT IF? GLASSES	DOOM AND GLOOM GLASSES
MAKE-BELIEVE GLASSES	MIND-READING GLASSES	I'M USELESS GLASSES
FORTUNE-TELLING GLASSES	I SHOULD GLASSES	I CAN'T GLASSES

What facts and evidence do I need to be aware of?

Are my thoughts based on these facts or evidence? Tick which answer applies to you.

a) Yes ☐ b) No ☐

Are my thoughts feeding or starving my Exam Stress Gremlin? Tick which answer applies to you.

a) Feeding ☐ b) Starving ☐

How can I think more realistically based on the facts and evidence in order to starve my Exam Stress Gremlin?

Here are some things to remember when challenging your negative and unrealistic thoughts about revision, exams and your ability to cope with them in order to starve your Exam Stress Gremlin:

- We are all worthy and equal.
- Perfection doesn't exist.
- Mistakes and weaknesses do not equal failure.
- We don't know what other people are thinking.
- Other people's opinions are not facts.
- We can't please everyone all of the time.
- The past doesn't have to equal the present or the future.
- Learning can be enjoyable.
- There will be positives in your life.
- It's OK to be different.
- We need to be true to our 'real' selves.
- We need to see the bigger picture of ourselves.

We Are All Worthy and Equal

Many people with exam stress have low self-confidence or self-esteem and see themselves as unworthy or not as worthy as other people. However, just because someone is better at something than you, it doesn't make them a more worthy person than you or more important than you. It doesn't mean their contribution to this world is more valuable than yours. Everyone who exists on this planet is worthy and equal. You don't need to do well in an exam to create your self-worth because you are already a person of worth by the very fact that you exist.

Perfection Doesn't Exist

We all place expectations on ourselves and sometimes we try to live up to the expectations that other people have for us in order to please them, to make them like us or to try to fit in. For people suffering with exam stress, these can often involve expectations that are unrealistic and place too much pressure on them, such as 'I need to be perfect'. But we would never achieve this expectation because no one is good at everything. Perfection doesn't exist!

So, in order to starve your Exam Stress Gremlin, remind yourself that you can only ever do your best and achieve things that are realistic for you based on your strengths, abilities and current circumstances. And remember, perfection doesn't exist!

In the next Exam Stress Box, list any expectations that you place on yourself in relation to exams and revision that you now realise are unrealistic and then write down more realistic expectations for yourself.

EXAM STRESS BOX

MY UNREALISTIC EXPECTATIONS ABOUT EXAMS AND REVISION	ALTERNATIVE REALISTIC EXPECTATIONS

Mistakes and Weaknesses Do Not Equal Failure

We all make mistakes and we all have weaknesses. They are a normal part of being human. We must learn to accept that making mistakes and having weaknesses does not make us a failure. It just means we are human like everyone else! So, give yourself permission to make mistakes and forgive yourself when you make them – they are not the end of the world!

We Don't Know What Other People Are Thinking

Unless you have mind-reading super powers, you actually have no idea what other people are thinking about you and your abilities. And yet, we often worry about what other people think, and predict what they are thinking at times – we wear the Mind-reading Exam Stress Thinking Glasses! And when we are stressed about exams and doubting our own ability to succeed at them, we tend to think that other people are thinking negative things about us, such as he/she 'isn't clever enough to pass these exams'. But remember, we don't know what other people are thinking, and other people rarely judge you as harshly as you judge yourself. We are normally our own worst critics!

Other People's Opinions Are Not Facts

It's important to remember that even if someone does think or say something negative about you, it doesn't make it fact! For example, perhaps you fail a History exam and one of your classmates calls you 'useless'. It doesn't mean you are. That person has formed their own personal opinion about you, but that does not mean that they have objectively assessed your character based on fact. It is just their opinion. The fact is that you only failed one test, not that you are useless!

We Can't Please Everyone All of the Time

You can't please all of the people all of the time because you're not responsible for how other people feel. You can only control how you feel. Not pleasing others doesn't make you a bad person – and focusing more on what you want from your life doesn't either! In fact, doing the latter will help you to learn more about the 'real' you and be confident in yourself and your abilities – thus starving your Exam Stress Gremlin and coping better with revision and exams!

In the next Exam Stress Box, list at least five things that you want to achieve in the next year because you want to and not because you think other people would approve of them – and remember, these don't have to be related to exams or qualifications!

EXAM STRESS BOX

Things I want to achieve in the future

The Past Doesn't Have to Equal the Present or the Future

Past events are merely indicators of what happened at that point in our lives, not predictors of the future. It is important to think factually about the present instead of worrying about the past or trying to predict the future using your Fortune-telling Exam Stress Thinking Glasses!

And remember that you can't predict your whole future based on one past event! So just because you may have failed one Science exam in the past, it doesn't mean you are going to fail every exam you take from here on in!

But you can learn from past exams and previous revision methods that you have used. Think proactively about what went well and what you would have changed and how you can implement that this time round in your revision and exams.

Learning Can be Enjoyable

In the run up to exams, we can feel so under pressure that we forget that learning should be an enjoyable experience. So, try and remind yourself what is good and enjoyable about school, studying and the subjects you like, and when you feel yourself struggling, think of those things. And bring some fun into your revision somehow. It is important to get back or develop a love of learning – it will really help!

There Will be Positives in Your Life

When we are feeling under the pressure of exams, it is also easy to feel as if everything in life is going wrong and everything in life is rubbish. If you feel this way, it is important to think realistically about your life and look for the positives within it – I'm sure they will be there! Have a go at writing down some positives in your life in the following Exam Stress Box and regularly look at these when times feel tough.

EXAM STRESS BOX

Positives in my life

It's OK to be Different

Q. What do you think it would be like to live on this planet if everyone was exactly the same?

....
....
....

All of us are different and unique in many ways and that is how it is meant to be. We are all supposed to have different talents, skills, abilities, characteristics, traits, looks and so on. If we didn't, how would we be able to fill all the jobs that are needed in society? Because of this, comparing ourselves to others is a waste of time. We aren't all meant to be the same.

Intelligence doesn't come in one single form. It's not all about having a high IQ (intelligence quotient) or being gifted at Maths and English. As humans, we have 'multiple intelligences', which can include things such as practical intelligence and creative intelligence. So, your best friend may be great at languages and always gets A grades in language exams, but it doesn't mean you have to be the same. Your best skill may be in sports or drama or photography – and that is just as fantastic!

Celebrate who you are and what you are good at – and don't ever feel that you aren't good enough! This will help you to starve your Exam Stress Gremlin!

We Must be True to Our 'Real' Selves

It is important to be true to your 'real' self and not to the kind of person others think you should be. Yes it is important to try your hardest in your exams, but you don't need to try and get top grades in all your academic subjects if that is unrealistic for you and puts too much pressure on you. You just need to:

- recognise the 'real' you
- accept the 'real' you
- work on becoming the best version of the 'real' you that you can and that is realistic for you
- be proud of you!

We Need to See the Bigger Picture of Ourselves

You cannot define yourself solely on one perceived weakness in a subject at school or college or on one exam result. Yes, your weaknesses make up part of who you are, but so do all your positive characteristics, traits, talents, skills and abilities. And yes, we all have them and you are no exception! You will have achieved many different things in your life that you can be proud of too!

Yes, it's important to work hard at your exams, but exam grades aren't the be all and end all that we can think they are. They have an impact on our futures, but they are just one of many factors that do. Other achievements, skills and qualities can be just as important in determining our future success and happiness, and employers also look for a wide range of skills and characteristics that aren't related to exam results.

It is therefore important always to focus on the bigger picture about yourself instead of just on one or two specific aspects. It's not about looking at yourself through rose-tinted glasses for the sake of it. It's about looking at yourself positively, based on what is factual and therefore realistic.

Here are some activities to help you to do this. You may struggle to complete some of these activities at first if your confidence and self-esteem are low, but it is important to keep working on them if you have the time, as they will help you to starve your Exam Stress Gremlin, keep your revision and exams in perspective and believe in yourself and your abilities!

In the next Exam Stress Box, list at least ten positive things about yourself and write down a piece of evidence to back up each statement. These could be positive qualities and characteristics, things you are good at, and your strengths, skills and talents. To give you an example, here are two things that Vaclav, aged 11 years, said about himself with accompanying evidence:

- 'I am a good and kind person because I help my blind grandma do her shopping every week.'
- 'I am a good singer because I got picked for the school choir.'

EXAM STRESS BOX

POSITIVES ABOUT ME	SUPPORTING EVIDENCE

Now list at least three things you have achieved in your life so far and write down at least one positive thing that each achievement shows you about yourself in the next Exam Stress Box.

EXAM STRESS BOX

MY ACHIEVEMENTS	POSITIVE THINGS THEY SHOW ABOUT ME

It can be helpful to keep a daily achievements diary in which you record things you have achieved that day and what they show you about yourself.

Finally, based on everything you've come up with so far, write down five positive statements about yourself in the next Exam Stress Box. We call these...

positive affirmations.

To help you with this, here are Vaclav's positive affirmations:

- 'I am a worthy person.'
- 'I am a good grandson.'
- 'I am a kind person.'
- 'I am a helpful person.'
- 'I am a creative person.'

EXAM STRESS BOX

My positive affirmations

Remind yourself of these regularly. Say them out loud. Put them somewhere you will see them every day. You can even send yourself a daily email or text with them written out!

Thinking about all the positive and realistic things about yourself in this way will help you to challenge your unrealistic and overly negative thoughts and to develop more positive and realistic ones. By recognising all these positives, you will learn to place less importance on your weaknesses as determining factors in your self-worth and by doing so you will be able to:

- more easily recognise what makes a good person and a successful person
- accept yourself for who you are and be proud of yourself
- be more confident in you and your abilities
- keep exams and their importance in perspective
- feel less pressure around exam time
- starve your Exam Stress Gremlin!

Using Visualisation

Another great way of thinking differently to help you keep calm, be positive and starve your Exam Stress Gremlin is to use something called...

visualisation.

This can involve picturing something in your head or thinking of memories that make you feel happy or relaxed or that make you laugh. Or you can picture yourself in a happy place. This can help you to feel calm at times when you are struggling under the pressure of revision or when you are feeling really nervous or anxious prior to or during an exam.

Another way in which you can use visualisation is to imagine what exam success would look like and picture yourself achieving it. This is a technique that sports people use to help motivate themselves mentally. For example, a runner might visualise themselves using the best possible running technique and winning their race in a personal best! You can also think about the things you feel will be difficult in your exams and picture yourself tackling those difficulties and how you would do it so you can feel prepared and more confident in your abilities.

You can also visualise all your worries and stresses being put in the bin or floating away like those leaves we talked about earlier. Or you can think of your negative and unrealistic thoughts as bubbles or balloons and imagine yourself popping them!

Now that you have learned about a number of different ways in which you can change how you think in order to starve your Exam Stress Gremlin and reduce your exam stress, it's time to focus on how you can also act differently to achieve the same results – which is what the next chapter is all about.

8

Starving the Exam Stress Gremlin

Acting Differently!

In Chapter 4, we learned that we act in ways that aren't good for us when we are experiencing exam stress and that these self-defeating behaviours feed our Exam Stress Gremlins and make our exam stress worse.

But we don't have to act in these ways. We can choose to act differently, by:

- reducing our self-defeating behaviours
- implementing more constructive behaviours.

Acting differently is step seven in starving your Exam Stress Gremlin and will help you to get rid of exam stress for good!

Remember, you don't have to try all the different strategies that you learn in this chapter. You only need to apply those that are relevant to you.

Reducing Self-Defeating Behaviours

The first way to change how you act is to reduce the behaviours that aren't good for you.

STOP AVOIDING!

Many people with exam stress avoid, quit or escape from exam- or revision-related situations in some way. But when you face these situations instead, you give yourself the opportunity to see that there is a difference between how you think and feel about a situation and what actually happens in it. For example, you get to:

- see that the negative outcomes that you are predicting are unlikely to come true
- achieve those things that you keep telling yourself you can't, thus allowing your confidence to grow

- see that you can cope even if your worst-case scenario does happen.

Therefore, it is important to ***gradually*** put yourself into the situations that you would normally avoid, quit or escape from due to your exam stress, and eventually your stress will gradually reduce.

But, take it step by step. Start with tasks or situations that seem easiest, such as revising at home, and only move on to the next step, such as attending a school revision club, when you feel ready. Accept that you will feel some worry, fear or stress at first, as that is normal, but remind yourself that it will pass. If you feel unable to do one of the actions, try breaking it down into smaller steps and tackle those bit by bit. It is OK to need to repeat a step several times until you feel completely comfortable with it. If you are struggling to motivate yourself to complete any of the steps, remind yourself why you need to, the benefits it will bring and that it will be OK. Use the realistic thinking techniques that you learned in the previous chapter, along with other behavioural strategies that you will learn later in this chapter (for example, relaxation techniques) to help you along the way. Finally, reward and praise yourself for achieving each step.

STOP PROCRASTINATING!

We often put off doing part of or all of our revision when suffering with exam stress and waste time doing other things instead, like watching TV. When we put off doing something, we call this...

procrastination.

Just like avoidance, procrastination stops us from seeing that things aren't as bad as we think they are and from realising that we can cope and achieve! In order to starve your Exam Stress Gremlin, you need to reduce procrastination by:

- thinking realistically and positively about revising and your ability to revise using the techniques that you learned in the previous chapter
- stopping making excuses for why you can't start or complete your revision
- visualising yourself successfully achieving your revision
- starting the revision task(s) that you are putting off
- setting yourself a step-by-step revision plan containing realistic and achievable steps, and tackling each step one at a time
- reducing the opportunity to get distracted by other things
- reminding yourself of the disadvantages of procrastination, such as not giving yourself enough time to revise everything you need to
- reminding yourself of the advantages of reducing procrastination, such as allowing yourself to see that you can achieve what you need to achieve
- reminding yourself of times when you didn't procrastinate and how well it went
- rewarding yourself along the way for completing steps on your revision plan!

DON'T STUDY TO EXCESS!

Some young people experiencing exam stress will be so caught up with trying to be perfect that they will study and revise to excess and end up burnt out before exam time arrives! But as you learned in the previous chapter, perfection doesn't exist! So:

- remember that it is impossible to achieve perfection
- set yourself expectations and goals that are realistic for you
- accept that if you don't achieve a goal, it isn't the end of the world
- remember that it is OK to make mistakes sometimes
- recognise that you cannot control everything in life or please everyone all of the time
- work hard but not to excess
- be proud of yourself and your achievements.

REDUCE OTHER SELF-DEFEATING BEHAVIOURS

This would be an incredibly long workbook if I was to go through everything that is needed to tackle all the other self-defeating behaviours that were listed in Chapter 4, such as:

- seeking reassurance from others or needing to be around others for comfort
- compulsive behaviours or rituals
- aggressive, defiant, disruptive or risk-taking behaviours
- restless behaviours
- using negative coping strategies, such as drinking, self-harming or binge eating.

However, setting yourself a gradual plan for reducing the frequency and amount of the behaviour that you want to tackle is a good place to start. And the following are some strategies that can help with this.

DITCH THOSE TOOLS!

Reduce the opportunity to perform the behaviour by removing the tools you need to achieve it. For example if you wish to reduce binge eating, stop buying the foods you would binge on.

DISTRACT YOURSELF!

Distract yourself from performing the behaviour by doing something else instead. The best forms of distraction are things that you enjoy doing, things that give you a sense of achievement and things that really absorb your attention.

DELAY, DELAY, DELAY!

Wait a little while before you start to perform the behaviour, as by waiting, even for just five minutes, it can reduce the urge to perform the behaviour. You are showing yourself that you have a choice over whether and when you perform this behaviour. You can also use the delay time to work on challenging any negative or unrealistic thoughts using the realistic thinking methods from the previous chapter!

SAY 'STOP'!

Say a trigger word such as 'stop!' to yourself when you feel the urge to perform the behaviour. This gives you the opportunity to challenge any negative or unrealistic thoughts using the realistic thinking methods discussed in the previous chapter.

SET LIMITS!

Place limits on your behaviours to restrict them in some way. This can include setting limits for the number of times you perform the behaviour in a day or a week or for the amount of time you spend performing the behaviour. It can also include only allowing yourself to perform the behaviour at a set time each day and if you miss that time you have to wait till the next day.

RESISTANCE!

Resist the urge to perform the behaviour completely. You may be able to do this straight away for behaviours that you don't believe are as vital or that you haven't been doing for as long. But for those you have the strongest urge for, you may have to build up to this more gradually using some of the other techniques above.

OUT WITH THE OLD AND IN WITH THE NEW!

Replace the behaviour with a more constructive way of acting, such as those we will look at in the rest of this chapter.

IS IT WORTH IT?

Write yourself a list of the advantages and disadvantages of performing the behaviour.

You are likely to feel increased levels of worry or fear or stress at first when trying to reduce your behaviours in these ways. But this is normal and will gradually diminish, especially if you implement one or more of the constructive behaviours that we will look at in the rest of this chapter.

In the following Exam Stress Box, write down the self-defeating behaviours you want to reduce and how you plan on achieving this.

EXAM STRESS BOX

MY SELF-DEFEATING BEHAVIOURS	HOW I CAN REDUCE THEM

Implementing Constructive Behaviours

You can also change how you act by implementing more constructive behaviours – these are behaviours that can help you to:

- relax
- feel better physically, mentally and emotionally
- be more confident
- study more effectively
- cope with the pressure of exams
- starve your Exam Stress Gremlin
- feel less stressed!

The constructive behaviours that we are going to look at are:

- talking and asking for help
- using the 'stress time' technique
- completing an exam stress diary
- changing your self-talk
- relaxing and having fun!
- living healthily
- problem solving
- being motivated and not giving up
- using positive revision techniques
- dealing with the night before the exam
- having a good exam day!

But remember, you don't need to use them all. Only those that you believe will help you to starve your Exam Stress Gremlin!

Talking and Asking for Help

Talking with a person that you trust is an important way of managing your stress and starving your Exam Stress Gremlin as it can help you to:

Express how you are feeling and get help with dealing with negative emotions	Challenge your negative and unrealistic thoughts	Identify ways to solve problems or cope with situations

Talking also involves asking for help when you need to, such as:

- asking your teacher for help when you don't understand something that you are learning or when you are unsure about how to revise for a subject
- asking a parent for help with balancing all the different things you may have going on in your life alongside your exams.

Don't forget, you can also talk to a professional, such as a doctor, psychologist or counsellor, about your exam stress and the way it is affecting you either face to face or through a telephone helpline.

Using the 'Stress Time' Technique

'Stress time' is a specific time in the day that you can use to think, talk or write about the exam- and revision-related things that you are stressing over and how you can think and act differently to get this stress under control. But set a time limit, as the less time you spend on your exam stress, the less you feed your Exam Stress Gremlin!

You can also use this time to practise the mindfulness techniques discussed in the previous chapter and let your negative thoughts and feelings go!

Completing an Exam Stress Diary

Often writing about your exam stress can help you to challenge your negative and unrealistic thoughts and identify ways to act differently to help you manage your stress or resolve a problem you might be facing. An example diary can be found on the next pages. You could use this during your 'stress time'.

Exam Stress Diary

Write your answers to the questions in the spaces below.

Date . . . .

What triggered your exam stress today?

What were your thoughts?

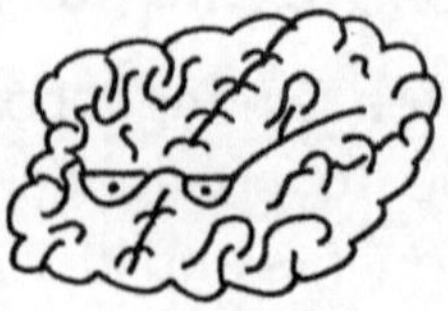

Did you think through Exam Stress Thinking Glasses? Tick which answer applies to you.

a) Yes ☐ b) No ☐

What physical stress reactions did you experience?

How did you feel emotionally?

How did you act?

Which of the following did you do? Tick which answer applies to you.

a) Starve your Exam Stress Gremlin ☐

b) Feed your Exam Stress Gremlin ☐

If you fed him, what could you have done differently to starve him?

If you starved him, well done!

Changing Your 'Self-Talk'

Your self-talk is how you talk about yourself. Being aware of how you talk about your abilities to revise for and perform in exams will help you to starve your Exam Stress Gremlin and get your exam stress under control. Your exam- and revision-related self-talk needs to be realistic and positive – just as your thoughts do. Have a go at answering the questions in the following Exam Stress Box to help you identify what your own self-talk is like and how you can change this for the better.

EXAM STRESS BOX

What words do you currently use when talking about your exam- and revision-related abilities?

....

....

What effects does your self-talk have on you?

....

....

How could you improve your self-talk?

....

....

....

....

Relaxing and Having Fun!

You can use simple relaxation and deep-breathing exercises to help you relax when you're feeling stressed about revision and exams. These can also be helpful when you are trying to face exam- and revision-related situations that you would normally avoid, or when you want to stop procrastinating or reduce other self-defeating behaviours as discussed earlier in this chapter.

Have a go at the following relaxation and breathing exercises and see what you think. It's OK if these don't feel right to you, as they aren't always suitable for everybody. But give them a go and see how you get on.

DEEP BREATHING EXERCISE 1

Either sit down or lie down on your back. Focus on your breathing. Put one hand on your upper chest and one on your abdomen (just below your ribs). Gently breathe in and, as you do so, notice that your abdomen rises slowly under your hand. Slowly breathe out noticing how your abdomen falls down slowly. Repeat the process, breathing in and out with a slow, steady rhythm. You are breathing correctly if your hand on your abdomen moves up and down slowly but the hand on your chest remains still.

DEEP BREATHING EXERCISE 2

Lie on your back. Breathe in deeply and slowly, imagining that the breath is coming in through the soles of your feet, travelling up through your body and exiting through your head. Breathe in again and this time imagine that the breath is coming in through your head, travelling down through your body and out through the soles of your feet. Repeat this exercise several times and slowly.

RELAXATION EXERCISE 1

Close your eyes and imagine yourself somewhere peaceful, happy or enjoyable. Somewhere that makes you feel relaxed and happy. Focus on that image, start to build the detail and, for a short time, imagine that you are actually there. Breathe deeply and slowly as you do.

RELAXATION EXERCISE 2

Focus on one muscle in your body at a time, and slowly tighten and then relax the muscle.

If the above activities aren't for you, you can always try other forms of activity or exercise that are aimed at relaxation, such as meditation, yoga and T'ai Chi. Alternatively, you can use activities that you enjoy to help you relax, such as:

- sports/exercise
- relaxing in a hot bath
- listening to or playing music
- watching TV
- spending time with friends or family
- volunteering
- reading
- going to the cinema
- other extra-curricular and leisure activities.

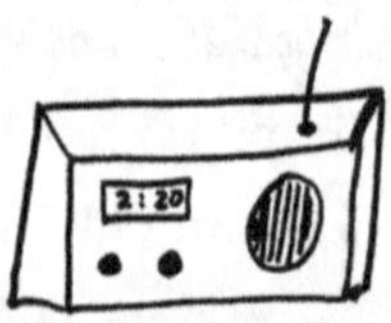

All the different types of activities mentioned in this section may also help to take your mind off the urge to perform self-defeating behaviours. In addition, they can be used as a reward when you achieve tasks on your revision plan so that you have something to look forward to! They can also provide a well-deserved break from everything related to exams and revision – as that is vital! And some of them may give you a chance to laugh – an important method for de-stressing and starving your Exam Stress Gremlin!

Have a go at coming up with a list of fun activities that you believe may work for you and write them down in the next Exam Stress Box.

EXAM STRESS BOX

My fun activities

Living Healthily

It is important to:

Eat a healthy balanced diet, have regular meals and reduce your sugar intake

Drink plenty of water, as our brains work better when properly hydrated. Reduce the amount of stimulants you drink like caffeine and sugary drinks

Exercise regularly, but not too much, and do stretches to help with the aches and pains of stress

Get enough quality sleep

These can help you to:

- feel better physically, such as calming down the negative physical reactions associated with stress, feeling more rested and increased energy levels
- be more positive
- concentrate better
- think more clearly
- feel more able to tackle the revision and exams that you need to do

- relax and feel calmer
- starve your Exam Stress Gremlin!

There are a number of strategies you can try if you are having trouble sleeping because of your exam stress. These are called...

sleep hygiene techniques.

SLEEP ENVIRONMENT

Look at what changes you may need to make to your sleep environment, such as noise levels, light levels, colours in the room, type of bed/mattress, heat levels and distractions in the room (for example, mobile phone or TV).

PRE-BED ROUTINE

Avoid anything too stimulating before bed. Do things that help you to relax instead. Empty your bladder. Write down any stressed thoughts or things that you might want to remember for the morning and deal with them in the morning.

SLEEP ROUTINE

Get up at approximately the same time and go to bed at approximately the same time each day.

EATING

Eat at regular times, as our body clock is also influenced by eating times.
Also avoid food too close to bedtime or stimulants like caffeine as they can disturb sleep patterns.

EXERCISE

Ensure you have done some physical activity in the day, but don't do aerobic exercise too close to bedtime as this will stimulate the system.

IF YOU CAN'T SLEEP

Get out of bed and do something relaxing and when you feel tired go back to bed and try to sleep again. Turn your clock to the wall as looking at it will only make you feel worse. Don't worry about not being able to sleep – this will only make things worse.

Problem Solving

Difficult situations and problems can occur in our lives. When it comes to exams and revision, types of problems might include:

- struggling with a particular subject
- not knowing enough about an exam or subject because you have been off school due to illness
- having difficulties finding quiet space in your house to revise
- having difficulties finding enough time to revise due to competing demands on your time, such as helping to care for a parent with an illness
- finding it difficult to say 'No' to unrealistic pressures and demands from others
- experiencing bullying because of your exam results.

However, stressing about these situations will not make them any better. Instead, you need to focus your energy on solving the problem you are facing in order to starve your Exam Stress Gremlin and reduce your stress levels. When working out how to tackle a problem you need to:

- identify exactly what the problem is
- think about possible solutions to the problem
- look at the pros and cons of each solution
- decide which approach to take and implement it.

Being Motivated and Not Giving Up!

When you are experiencing exam stress, it is easy to feel as if everything is too much and it is really hard to find the motivation to keep going. It can feel easier to just give up. But then you aren't giving yourself the opportunity to show yourself just how well you can do.

Even though it may feel too hard, it is important to keep going. You might not feel motivated to do so at first, but grit your teeth and make yourself tackle what's ahead of you. If you do, you will gradually feel more and more comfortable with what you are doing, you will feel proud of yourself, you will feel more confident and then the motivation to continue will kick in!

To help with your motivation, break your revision tasks into small chunks so they feel less daunting and keep reminding yourself of the benefits of keeping going and the disadvantages of giving up! The more motivated you are, the more you starve your Exam Stress Gremlin and the smaller and smaller he gets!

Using Positive Revision Techniques

A variety of practical revision techniques can help you to starve your Exam Stress Gremlin and manage your stress levels.

BE PREPARED!

Fear of the unknown can be a huge trigger for exam stress. So, make sure you know as much as you can about the practicalities of your exams, such as:

- venues
- timetable
- format of exam
- types of questions and question formats
- marking system
- equipment needed.

DO A REVISION PLAN!

Time management and organisation are key to doing well, so it's important to develop a revision plan and stick to it as best you can. This involves:

- making sure you start your revision as soon as you can
- breaking your revision up into small chunks
- ensuring your revision goals are realistic and achievable in the timescales you are giving yourself
- working on achieving each revision task, step by step
- revising in short bursts of 20–30 minutes at a time, as we remember things better if we do this
- planning your timetable around the times of day you revise best

- using short timeslots that you have here and there in your day – you don't have to wait until you have a full day to yourself to revise
- putting regular breaks and reward time into your revision plan
- prioritising your revision – sometimes you can't revise everything on a topic as you don't have time. So, ask your teachers for guidance and use past papers to help you work out what is most important to revise
- planning extra time into your revision timetable that you can use in case you have to miss a revision session due to illness or something takes you longer to revise than expected.

THE RIGHT STUDY ENVIRONMENT

Obviously, we have to work with what we have access to, but it's important to make the best of whatever study environment you have available. Where possible, have your study environment as a calm, quiet place that is free from distractions and organised in a way that works for you. Also make sure you have easy access to the equipment you need for your revision so you don't waste valuable revision time looking for things! Study in the place that works best for you!

LEARNING STYLES

There are different types of learning style, namely:

- Visual learning – where we learn through seeing
- Auditory learning – where we learn through hearing
- Kinaesthetic learning – where we learn through doing.

We tend to have a preference for one and it can be important to therefore use the way that you find most effective for you. But it can also be good to use different types as this can improve our ability to recall information as it gives our brains different ways of trying to remember and recall the information. Active learning methods where you have to keep practising your recall and not just reading something can be particularly effective. So why not combine some of the methods below so as to make your learning as active and varied as possible? But just use the ones that are most effective for you:

- Reading
- Thinking
- Drawing diagrams and mind maps
- Recording yourself speaking notes and listen to them
- Watching TV programmes, listening to podcasts or accessing websites or apps that relate to your revision
- Asking questions of yourself and getting others to ask you questions
- Explaining things out loud to yourself or others
- Answering past exam questions
- Writing summaries
- Taking part in a study group or school revision sessions
- Producing short revision notes/flash cards
- Producing revision posters or post-it notes for your bedroom, bathroom, kitchen – whichever location works best for you
- Applying what you are learning to real-life situations or things that interest you to aid recall
- Using mnemonics, rhymes or associations between the learning and something else.

BE PROUD OF YOUR ACHIEVEMENTS

It is very easy to focus on what you haven't achieved yet or to panic when you don't complete everything you wanted to in a revision session. But that will just feed your Exam Stress Gremlin and increase your stress levels! Instead, focus on all you have achieved and be proud of yourself.

Dealing with the Night Before the Exam!

Here are some tips to help you starve your Exam Stress Gremlin and keep calm the night before your exam:

- Only do minor revision – don't try and learn anything new.
- Make sure you finish your revision early enough to give yourself time to relax.
- Get some exercise.
- Eat well and drink plenty of water.
- Remind yourself of the positives about you and your life and keep the exam in perspective.
- Use the techniques learned throughout this workbook to help you keep calm.
- Have everything ready that you need for the exam, such as equipment and bottle of water.

- Make sure you know what time you need to be at the exam and where it is.
- Get an early night.
- Set your alarm!

Having a Good Exam Day!

Here are some tips to help you starve your Exam Stress Gremlin and keep calm on exam day:

- Eat a good breakfast and drink plenty of water.
- Wear something comfortable.
- Don't try to learn any new topics at the last minute as this will only panic you.
- Again, remind yourself of the positives about you and your life and keep the exam in perspective.

- Make sure you're not rushing or late as this will add to your stress. But don't arrive so early that you have too much time just to sit and get more and more nervous.
- Avoid people who seem stressed outside the exam room.
- Try to avoid revising for the last hour before the exam and instead focus on doing things to help you relax and keep calm.
- Go to the toilet prior to the exam starting.
- On entering the exam room, take a few minutes to calm and settle yourself before starting.

- If you are allowed to do so and if it's relevant to your type of exam, jot down any key things you want to remember or are afraid of forgetting in the margins of the paper before you start, and scribble them out at the end.
- Take the time to read the instructions and questions properly before answering so you are clear as to what you need to do.
- Skim through the whole paper so you know how to plan your time.
- Manage your time as effectively as you can so that you give yourself enough time for each question. If you are going to run out of time, don't be afraid to answer a question in note form as you are still likely to pick up some marks that way.

- Plan your answers where appropriate.
- Think about answering the questions you find easiest first so you can build your confidence, or the ones that will give you the most marks.
- If you find yourself panicking or getting too stressed, use some of the techniques that you have learned about already in this workbook to help you calm down and keep things in perspective. If you need to, ask to leave the exam room to go to the toilet, as just taking a break for a few minutes might be all you need.

- If your mind goes blank, don't panic. Take some deep breaths, remind yourself of just how much you know, jot down some notes to help stimulate your memory, or if you need to move on to a different question and return to the original one later in the exam when you are feeling more confident, then do so.
- Make sure your handwriting can be read.

- Show the processes that you use to work out your answers in subjects like Maths or Science as this can help you gain marks, even if your final answer is incorrect.
- Don't leave any questions blank, just have a go.
- Allow yourself time at the end of the exam to check over your answers.
- Don't worry about how quickly other people finish the exam – just focus on your own exam paper.
- Once finished, don't spend hours speculating about how you think you've done. Instead, reward yourself for doing the best you could by doing something relaxing and enjoyable, and be proud of yourself!

Well done! You have now learned so much to help you starve your Exam Stress Gremlin and get rid of your exam stress for good! Now it is about putting it all into practice at a pace and in a way that feels right for you!

9

Summing Up!

Congratulations! You have now learned what you need to know about exam stress and it's time to put it all into practice and take the final step towards starving your Exam Stress Gremlin! But don't forget, you may not need to use all the strategies we've looked at in this book. Just work on implementing those that are relevant to you and your own exam stress.

Remember, only you can change:

- how you think about exams
- how your body reacts physically as a result of your thoughts about exams
- how you feel emotionally in response to your thoughts about exams
- how you act in response to your thoughts and feelings about exams!

You're the one in control of your exam stress!
You have the power to starve your Exam Stress Gremlin and get rid of exam stress for good!

Before we finish, let's have a quick recap using some activities. If you don't have the time to complete them all due to your revision, don't worry. Just do what you can and what feels right in your own circumstances.

What Have You Learned?

First, write down five things you have learned about exam stress and how to control it in the next Exam Stress Box.

EXAM STRESS BOX

What have I learned?

Spread the Word on How to Starve the Exam Stress Gremlin!

Now have a go at a more creative way of reinforcing what you have learned with the following activity.

YOUR VOICE! (PART 2)

If you wanted to spread the word far and wide to other young people about exam stress and how to manage it, what would you do? Pick whether you would:

- design a webpage for young people to access
- write a blog aimed at young people
- design a poster campaign for schools and colleges
- design scenes for a TV advert
- give a talk at schools and colleges
- deliver a play at schools and colleges.

Then, in the space below, jot down ideas on the kinds of things you would include in whichever type of campaign method you would use. And if you want to have a go at completing your campaign advert or poster on some separate paper or a computer, go ahead. Just think, maybe your school or college might want to use it!

Teaching other young people about exam stress

Exam Stress Agony Aunt or Uncle

Imran is 11 years old. He is due to take some important exams. He can't stop thinking about the exams and he is petrified of not doing well enough. He thinks his friends will laugh at him if he doesn't do well and that he will disappoint his parents and upset his teachers. He is struggling to sleep at night, and when he does fall asleep he has nightmares about failing his exams. He is finding it hard to eat as his stomach feels as if it is always in knots. He sits down to revise every day after school and at weekends, but he never gets very far as he can't concentrate. Instead, he tells himself he is 'too stupid to pass the tests' and just sits at his desk staring into space. He cries a lot when he is in his bedroom and he has stopped going out to play with his friends.

What advice would you give Imran? Write your advice in the Exam Stress Box below.

EXAM STRESS BOX

Dear Imran

Exam Stress Changes

In the Exam Stress Box below, write down any changes you have seen in your exam stress since starting this workbook and what you think has led to these changes.

EXAM STRESS BOX

Changes in my exam stress and why

I hope that you have seen your exam stress levels start to reduce and that the way you are responding to exams and revision is starting to change too. As you continue to put everything you have learned from this workbook into practice, remember to be patient with yourself. You won't change everything overnight and no one gets it right all the time! Remember, no one is perfect! Here is one final activity to help you along the way!

Exam Stress Goals

In the Exam Stress Box below, write down any goals you would like to set yourself so you can continue to starve your Exam Stress Gremlin and keep your exam stress under control.

EXAM STRESS BOX

My exam stress goals

OK, here are just a few final words from me.

It is normal to feel nervous about exams. It is normal to experience a certain level of pressure in response to exams, but it is not healthy for you to get to the stage where it all feels too much and you feel stressed. Remember...

You are in control of how you respond to exams.

And stressing won't help – it will just make things worse.

You can starve your Exam Stress Gremlin and get rid of exam stress for good!

Just believe in you!

Keep as calm as you can and do your best. No one can ask any more of you than that!

And you will be surprised at just how well you do as a result!

Good luck with your revision, exams and starving your Exam Stress Gremlin!

This is to certify that

....

has successfully completed the
Starving the Exam Stress Gremlin
workbook and can expertly

STARVE THEIR
EXAM STRESS GREMLIN!

Information for Parents and Professionals

The Purpose of This Workbook

Starving the Exam Stress Gremlin provides a cognitive behavioural approach to managing exam stress for young people. It is designed for young people to work through on their own or with the support of a parent or a professional, such as a teacher, mentor, teaching assistant or youth worker.

The self-help materials included in this workbook are based on the principles of cognitive behavioural therapy (CBT) and mindfulness, but do not constitute a session-by-session therapeutic programme. However, the materials contained in this workbook can be used as a resource for therapists working with young people.

What is Cognitive Behavioural Therapy?

CBT is an evidence-based, skills-based, structured form of psychotherapy, which emerged from Beck's Cognitive Therapy (Beck 1976) and Ellis' Rational-Emotive Therapy (Ellis 1962), as well as from the work of behaviourists such as Pavlov (Pavlov 1927) and Skinner (Skinner 1938) on classical and operant conditioning, respectively. CBT looks at the relationships between our thoughts (cognition), our feelings (both physical and emotional) and our actions (behaviours). It is based on the premise that how we interpret experiences and situations has a profound effect on our physical, emotional and behavioural reactions.

CBT focuses on:

- the problems that the client is experiencing in the here and now
- why the problems are occurring
- what strategies the client can use in order to address the problems.

In doing so, the CBT process empowers the client to identify:

- negative, unhealthy and unrealistic patterns of thoughts, perspectives and beliefs
- maladaptive and unhealthy patterns of behaviour
- the links between the problems the client is facing and his or her patterns of thoughts and behaviours
- how to challenge the existing patterns of thoughts and behaviours and implement alternative thoughts and behaviours that are constructive, healthy and realistic in order to address problems, manage emotions and improve well-being.

Thus the underlying ethos of CBT is that by addressing unhelpful patterns of thoughts and behaviours, a person can change how they feel, how they view themselves, how they interact with others and how they approach life in general – thereby moving from an unhealthy cycle of reactions to a healthy one.

A wide range of empirical studies show CBT to be effective with many mental health disorders, including:

- anxiety (Cartwright-Hatton *et al.* 2004; James, Soler and Weatherall 2005)
- obsessive compulsive disorder (OCD) (O'Kearney *et al.* 2006)
- depression (Klein, Jacobs and Reinecke 2007).

Furthermore, guidelines published by the National Institute for Health and Care Excellence (NICE) recommend the use of CBT for a number of mental health issues, including depression (NICE 2005a) and OCD (NICE 2005b).

Effectiveness of CBT for Children and Young People

Although there has been less research conducted on the use of CBT with children and young people than there has been with adults, evidence for its effectiveness is continuing to grow and is reported in a number of reviews, such as Kazdin and Weisz (1998) and Rapee *et al.* (2000). Random clinical trials have shown CBT to be effective with children and young people for the following:

- specific phobias (Silverman *et al.* 1999)
- generalised anxiety disorder (Kendall *et al.* 1997, 2004)
- social phobia (Spence, Donovan and Brechman-Toussaint 2000)
- obsessive compulsive disorder (Barrett, Healy-Farrell and March 2004)
- school refusal (King *et al.* 1998)
- depression (Lewinsohn and Clarke 1999).

What is Mindfulness?

Mindfulness originates from spiritual disciplines such as Buddhism and from practices such as meditation and yoga. The essence of mindfulness is that we can make a choice to:

- focus our attention on the present moment, thus engaging fully in the here and now with all our senses
- accept our thoughts and feelings as they are, thus observing them without criticism or judgement
- let those thoughts and feelings go, thus reducing any negative impact.

In the 1970s, mindfulness principles and practices were incorporated into a form of training known as mindfulness-based stress reduction (MBSR) developed by Jon Kabat-Zinn. In the 1990s, principles of mindfulness also emerged within psychotherapy and became known as mindfulness-based cognitive therapy (MBCT) for use with people with a history of depression.

The key principles of mindfulness detailed above are also now incorporated into acceptance and commitment therapy (ACT), a mindfulness and values-based form of behavioural therapy. ACT sees our 'private experiences' (namely our thoughts, feelings and physical sensations) as not harmful in themselves. What is seen as harmful within ACT is how we choose to respond to those private experiences, such as seeing them as reality (what ACT terms 'cognitive fusion') and avoiding experiencing these thoughts, feelings and physical sensations (known as experiential avoidance). Thus, as well as teaching us principles of acceptance and being fully present in the moment, ACT also teaches us to make a distinction between our 'private experiences' and reality (a process known as 'cognitive defusion') and to commit to action that enriches and nourishes our lives based on our values (known as values-consistent behaviours).

The empirical support for ACT as an effective form of treatment for mental health issues such as anxiety and depression is growing (Forman *et al.* 2007).

Effectiveness of Mindfulness-Based Therapies for Children and Young People

Research on the use of mindfulness-based therapies with children and young people is still in its infancy. However, evidence supporting its use is growing, especially in relation to ACT (for example, Greco *et al.* 2005; Murrell and Scherbarth 2006). Studies are showing support for the use of ACT for children and young people with depression (Hayes, Boyd and Sewell 2011), generalised anxiety disorder (Greco 2002), anorexia nervosa (Heffner, Sperry and Eifert 2002) and pain (Greco *et al.* under review). And research is beginning to highlight how ACT can help to address the links between body image concerns and disordered eating in young people (Greco and Blomquist 2006). Research is also emerging suggesting that mindfulness-based approaches can have positive impacts in relation to students' anxiety, as you will see later in this section.

Exam Stress

Previously, research and discussion on exam stress stemmed mainly from America. However, it is becoming more prevalent internationally just as exam stress itself is on the rise. For example, a 2015 UK study for the National Union of Teachers (Hutchings 2015) found that 90 per cent of the teachers surveyed reported pupils becoming very stressed and anxious prior to exams, and studies such as those by Owen-Yeates (2005) and McDonald (2001) have found that children and young people commonly report exams as stressful, worrying and fear-provoking.

Recent academic studies have focused more on the construct of 'test anxiety' – which occurs where a person experiences a situation-specific form of anxiety in response to their performance being evaluated by others through an exam – rather than 'exam stress' in general. This is mainly because test anxiety is seen as a more measurable construct for robust empirical research (it is measured for research purposes by self-reporting scales such as the Test Anxiety Inventory (Spielberger 1980), the Children's Test Anxiety Questionnaire (Wren and Benson 2004) or the Revised Test Anxiety Scale (Benson *et al.* 1992)), but there are clear similarities and crossovers between the two constructs.

Estimates for the prevalence of test anxiety and exam stress vary widely. However, empirical studies clearly suggest that test anxiety is increasing, and surveys such as those by ChildLine (NSPCC 2015b), the Scout Association (2007) and Girl Guides Association (2008), as well as statistics on counselling sessions conducted by ChildLine (NSPCC 2014, 2015a, 2016) (as discussed in Chapter 6 of this workbook), clearly show that exam stress in general is on the rise too. Research is also showing that female students, students with disabilities and minority students report higher rates of test anxiety (Harlen and Deakin Crick 2002; Putwain 2007; Rosairio *et al.* 2008; Sena, Lowe and Lee 2007). However, it is clear that exam stress can affect a wide range of pupils, including both high and low attaining students (Hutchings 2015). Studies also show that test anxiety can occur as early as seven years of age (Connor 2003; Putwain 2008), which is certainly true in the UK where children now take Standard Attainment Tests (SATs) at six and seven years of age as well as at ten and eleven years of age.

Many empirical studies attribute the increase in exam stress and test anxiety to a corresponding increase in the use of high-stakes testing (McCaleb-Kahan and Wenner 2009; McDonald 2001; Putwain 2008; Segool 2009; Tymms and Merrell 2007). The studies highlight how high-stakes examinations can often produce higher levels of test anxiety than everyday classroom tests (for example, Segool 2009; Segool *et al.* 2013) and how many students now see education as being purely about exams and qualifications as opposed to gaining a rounded education that develops the whole child, fosters individuality, creativity and a love for learning, and values a wide range of skills (Hutchings 2015).

Studies have also focused on how student perceptions of lower competence predict higher test anxiety (Bonaccio and Reeve 2010; Chamorro-Premuzic, Ahmetoglu and Furnham 2008; Goetz *et al.* 2008; King and Ollendick 1989; Putwain and Daniels 2010; Putwain, Woods and Symes 2010), and how, for students with lower academic efficacy, emphasising the importance of tests can increase anxiety levels (Nie, Lau and Liau 2011). In relation to the latter, research is increasingly focusing on the use of 'fear appeals' (messages used by teachers to emphasise test importance and/or the consequences of test failure) in classrooms and their negative impacts, including higher levels of test anxiety (Connor 2001, 2003; Hall *et al.* 2004; Hutchings 2015; Putwain and Best 2011, 2012; Putwain and Roberts 2009; Putwain and Symes 2011). Putwain and Remedios (2014) also found that such fear messages can lead to decreased motivation and poorer exam performance when used frequently and when students perceive them to be threatening.

Both pupil surveys and empirical studies alike report students being worried about letting other people down due to the pressure that can be put on them to achieve by some parents and the implications of their results for the reputations of their teachers and their school (Connors *et al.* 2009; Hutchings 2015; NSPCC 2014, 2015a, 2015b, 2016), and about the effects of their exam results on their futures (Connors *et al.* 2009; Hutchings 2015; NSPCC 2014), with this even applying to children as young as ten years of age (Kellogg's 2015). Pupils also report being worried about their peers laughing at them or bullying them because of their results (NSPCC 2014) and how some of their peers boast about results, making them feel under more pressure themselves (Hutchings 2015). Students' perceptions of self-worth are becoming increasingly bound up with exam results as a result of the aforementioned areas (Connors *et al.* 2009), and they are gaining a 'greater awareness at younger ages of their [students'] own "failure"' (Hutchings 2015, p.5), thus leading to increased stress levels.

Empirical studies on test anxiety also highlight its cognitive, behavioural, physiological and emotional symptoms (for example, Zeidner and Mathews 2005) and how these symptoms can have a negative impact on a student's exam performance and, therefore, on their academic careers (Cizek and Burg 2006; Hembree 1988; McDonald 2001; Segool *et al.* 2013; Sena, Lowe and Lee 2007). Connors *et al.* (2009) found this to be particularly the case for children with poorer resilience. This impact on exam success is often attributed to anxious thoughts interfering with the student's ability to perform the cognitive tasks necessary for revision and completing the exam itself, such as memory recall, concentration, question reading and comprehension (Eysenck *et al.* 2007; King, Ollendick and Gullome 1991; Owens *et al.* 2008), with the stressed/ anxious thinking causing an almost 'cognitive overload'.

Other studies have focused on the impacts of the distorted and negative thinking involved in test anxiety on students' performance. For example, Putwain (2009) discussed how students with test anxiety get stuck in a 'debilitating cycle of catastrophic thinking' relating to predicting failure, which is increased further if a student has difficulties answering questions due to the other cognitive, behavioural, physical and emotional symptoms involved in test anxiety as this increases the likelihood of poorer performance, which then reinforces negative thinking even further. Similar results on the impact of distorted and negative thinking patterns have also been found in further studies by Putwain (Putwain, Connors and Symes 2010).

Exam stress brings with it a wide range of symptoms and impacts (as you will see in Chapters 3 to 5 of this workbook). For example, Hutchings (2015) found that both teachers and pupils reported lowered motivation and confidence as negative impacts of testing for some pupils, especially those who struggle to perform at the level they would like. One pupil explained how getting low marks 'makes people that aren't as good and don't have enough confidence in themselves less confident' (p.58). This was echoed in a survey by the Girl Guides Association (2008) where almost a fifth of respondents reported exams making them 'feel bad about themselves'. Teachers surveyed and interviewed in the study by Hutchings (2015) also reported students self-harming and missing school, experiencing panic attacks, depression and eating disorders, and having perfectionist beliefs. One teacher described having witnessed ten and eleven year olds in 'complete meltdown', and a pupil described how some fellow pupils would be crying for most of the exam because they were so stressed out (Hutchings 2015). ChildLine reviews and various young people surveys report similar signs and symptoms, as well as using drugs and alcohol as coping mechanisms, and sleep disturbance issues (Girl Guides Association 2008; Kellogg's 2015; NSPCC 2014, 2015a, 2015b, 2016; The Prince's Trust 2013). Furthermore, ChildLine (NSPCC 2013, p.37) reported that 'the pressure and stress of exams and not being able to deal with failure was another reason young people wanted to escape, seeing suicide as their only option'.

CBT and Exam Stress

More research needs to be done on the effectiveness of both treatment and prevention models for exam stress or test anxiety. However, a meta-analysis by Ergene (2003) and a systematic review of treatment studies (such as those studied by Weems *et al.* (2009) and Gregor (2005)) by von der Embse, Barterian and Segool (2013) found that cognitive behavioural approaches provide promising results. This is supported by research by Fayand, Badri Gargari and Sarandi (2013), which found that cognitive therapy training methods are effective in reducing test anxiety, and by Karkhaneh and Yazdanbakhsh (2015), which found that cognitive behavioural training interventions are effective. Furthermore, Reiss *et al.* (2017) found that pairing a cognitive behavioural intervention with techniques such as relaxation methods and imagery rescripting is also effective in reducing test anxiety.

Mindfulness and Exam Stress

Research into the effectiveness of mindfulness-based approaches for treating or preventing exam stress is in its infancy. But emerging studies are showing positive results. For example, Cho *et al.* (2016) found that mindful breathing reduced test anxiety; Mrazek *et al.* (2013) found that mindfulness training improved cognitive functioning in areas such as reducing mind-wandering and improving working memory capacity; and Dundas *et al.* (2016) found that mindfulness-based stress reduction had a positive impact on reducing evaluation anxiety.

References

Barrett, P., Healy-Farrell, L. and March, J.S. (2004) 'Cognitive-behavioural family treatment of childhood obsessive compulsive disorder: A controlled trial.' *Journal of the American Academy of Child and Adolescent Psychiatry, 43*, 1, 46–62.

Beck, A.T. (1976) *Cognitive Therapy and Emotional Disorders.* New York: International Universities Press.

Benson, J., Moulin-Julian, M., Schwarzer, C., Seipp, B. and El-Zahhar, N. (1992) 'Cross Validation of a Revised Test Anxiety Scale Using Multi-National Samples' In K.A. Hagvet and T.B. Johnsen (eds) *Advances in Test Anxiety Research*, Volume 7. Amsterdam: Swets & Zeitlinger.

Bonaccio, S. and Reeve, C. (2010) 'The nature and relative importance of students' perceptions of the sources of test anxiety.' *Learning and Individual Differences, 20*, 617–625.

Cartwright-Hatton, S., Roberts, C., Chitsabesan, P., Fothergill, C. and Harrington, R. (2004) 'Systematic review of the efficacy of cognitive behaviour therapies for childhood and adolescent anxiety disorders.' *British Journal of Clinical Psychology, 43*, 421–436.

Chamorro-Premuzic, T., Ahmetoglu, G. and Furnham, A. (2008) 'Little more than personality: Dispositional determinants of test anxiety (the big five, core self-evaluations and self-assessed intelligence). *Learning and Individual Differences, 18*, 2, 258–263.

Cho, H., Ryu, S., Noh, J. and Lee, J. (2016) 'The effectiveness of daily mindful breathing practices on test anxiety of students.' *PLoS One, 11*, 10.

Cizek, G.J. and Burg, S.S. (2006) *Addressing Test Anxiety in a High-Stakes Environment: Strategies for Classrooms and Schools.* Thousand Oaks, CA: Corwin Press.

Connor, M.J. (2001) 'Pupil stress and standardised assessment tests (SATs).' *Emotional and Behavioural Difficulties, 6*, 103–111.

Connor, M.J. (2003) 'Pupil stress and standard assessment tasks (SATs): An update.' *Emotional and Behavioural Difficulties, 8*, 2, 101–107.

Connors, L., Putwain, D.W., Woods, K. and Nicholson, L. (2009) 'Paper 3. Causes and consequences of test anxiety in Key Stage 2 pupils: The mediational role of emotional resilience.' Examination Anxiety in Primary, Secondary and Sixth Form Students, Symposium presented at the British Educational Research Association Conference, 2–5 September 2009. Available at: www.leeds.ac.uk/educol/documents/184268.pdf, accessed 23 November 2016.

Dundas, I., Thorsheim, T., Hjeltnes, A. and Binder, P.E. (2016) 'Mindfulness-based stress reduction for academic evaluation anxiety: A naturalistic longitudinal study.' *Journal of College Student Psychotherapy, 30*, 2, 114–131.

Ellis, A. (1962) *Reason and Emotion in Psychotherapy.* New York: Lyle-Stuart.

Ergene, T. (2003) 'Effective interventions on test anxiety reduction.' *School Psychology International, 24*, 3, 313–328.

Eysenck, M.W., Santos, R., Derekeshan, N. and Calvo, M.G. (2007) 'Anxiety and cognitive performance: Attentional control theory.' *Emotion, 7*, 336–353.

Fayand, J., Badri Gargari, R. and Sarandi, P. (2013) 'An investigation of the effects of cognitive therapy training on test anxiety in secondary education.' *European Journal of Experimental Biology, 3*, 1, 116–120.

Forman, E.M., Hoffman, K.L., McGrath, K.B., Herbert, J.D., Brandsma, L.L. and Lowe, M.R. (2007) 'A comparison of acceptance- and control-based strategies for coping with food cravings: An analog study.' *Behaviour Research and Therapy, 45*, 1, 2372–2386.

Girl Guides Association (2008) *Teenage Mental Health: Girls Shout Out!* Available at: https://www.mentalhealth.org.uk/sites/default/files/a-generation_0.pdf, accessed 25 July 2017.

Goetze, T., Preckel, F., Zeidner, M. and Schleyer, E. (2008) 'Big fish in big ponds: A multilevel analysis of test anxiety and achievement in special gifted classes.' *Anxiety, Stress and Coping, 21*, 2, 185–198.

Greco, L.A. (2002) 'Creating a context of acceptance in child clinical and paediatric settings.' Paper presented at the annual meeting of the Association for the Advancement of Behavior Therapy, Reno, NV.

Greco, L.A. and Blomquist, K.K. (2006) 'Body Image, Eating Behaviour, and Quality of Life Among Adolescent Girls: Role of Anxiety and Acceptance Processes in a School Sample.' In K.S. Berlin and A.R. Murrell (co-chairs) *Extending Acceptance and Mindfulness Research to Parents, Families and Adolescents: Process, Empirical Findings, Clinical Implications and Future Directions.* Symposium conducted at the Association for Behavior and Cognitive Therapies, Chicago, IL.

Greco, L.A., Blackledge, J.T., Coyne, L.W. and Ehrenreich, J. (2005) 'Integrating Acceptance and Mindfulness into Treatments for Child and Adolescent Anxiety Disorders: Acceptance and Commitment Therapy as an Example.' In S.M. Orsillo and L. Roemer (eds) *Acceptance and Mindfulness-Based Approaches to Anxiety: Conceptualization and Treatment.* New York: Springer Science.

Greco, L.A., Blomquist, K.K., Acra, S. and Moulton, D. (under review) 'Acceptance and commitment therapy for adolescents with functional abdominal pain: Results of a pilot investigation.' Manuscript submitted for publication. As cited in L.A. Greco and S.C. Hayes (2008) *Acceptance and Mindfulness Treatments for Children and Adolescents: A Practitioner's Guide.* Oakland, CA: New Harbinger Publications.

Gregor, A. (2005) 'Examination anxiety: Live with it, control it or make it work for you?' *School Psychology International, 26*, 617–635.

Hall, K., Collins, C., Benjamin, S., Nind, M. and Sheehy, K. (2004) 'SATurated models of pupildom: Assessment and inclusion/exclusion.' *British Educational Research Journal, 30*, 801–818.

Harlen, W. and Deakin Crick, R. (2002) *A Systematic Review of the Impact of Summative Assessment and Tests on Students' Motivation for Learning.* EPPI-Centre Review. London: EPPI-Centre, Social Science Research Unit, Institute of Education.

Hayes, L., Boyd, C.P. and Sewell, J. (2011) 'Acceptance and commitment therapy for the treatment of adolescent depression: A pilot study in a psychiatric outpatient setting.' *Mindfulness, 2*, 2, 86–94.

Heffner, M., Sperry, J. and Eifert, G.H. (2002) 'Acceptance and commitment therapy in the treatment of an adolescent female with anorexia nervosa: A case example.' *Cognitive and Behavioural Practice, 9*, 3, 232–236.

Hembree, R. (1988) 'Correlates, causes, effects and treatment of test anxiety.' *Review of Educational Research, 58*, 47–77.

Hutchings, M. (2015) *Exam Factories? The Impact of Accountability Measures on Children and Young People.* Research commissioned by the National Union of Teachers. London: London Metropolitan University.

James, A.A.C.J., Soler, A. and Weatherall, R.R.W. (2005) 'Cognitive behavioural therapy for anxiety disorders in children and adolescents.' *Cochrane Database of Systematic Reviews 2005*, Issue 4. Art. No.: CD004690. DOI:10.1002/14651858.CD004690.pub2. Published online January 2009.

Karkhaneh, M. and Yazdanbakhsh, K. (2015) 'Effectiveness of cognitive-behavioural intervention training method in reducing exam anxiety in teenagers.' *Indian Journal of Fundamental and Applied Life Sciences, 5*, 2, 2844–2851.

Kazdin, A.E. and Weisz, J.R. (1998) 'Identifying and developing empirically supported child and adolescent treatments.' *Journal of Consulting and Clinical Psychology, 66*, 19–36.

Kellogg's (2015) 'SATs anxiety: 10- and 11-year-olds worry that failing exams will affect their futures.' *Kellogg's Press Office News Release*, 11 May 2015. Available at: http://pressoffice.kelloggs.co.uk/SATS-ANXIETY-10-AND-11-YEAR-OLDS-WORRY-THAT-FAILING-EXAMS-WILL-AFFECT-THEIR-FUTURES, accessed 23 November 2016.

Kendall, P.C., Flannery-Schroeder, E., Panichelli-Mindel, S.M., Sotham-Gerow, M., Henin, A. and Warman, M. (1997) 'Therapy with youths with anxiety disorders: A second randomized clinical trial.' *Journal of Consulting and Clinical Psychology, 18*, 255–270.

Kendall, P.C., Safford, S., Flannery-Schroeder, E. and Webb, A. (2004) 'Child anxiety treatment: Outcomes in adolescence and impact on substance abuse and depression at 7.4 year follow-up.' *Journal of Consulting and Clinical Psychology, 72*, 276–287.

King, N.J. and Ollendick, T.H. (1989) 'Children's anxiety and phobic disorders in school settings: Classification, assessment and intervention issues.' *Review of Educational Research, 59*, 4, 431–470.

King, N.J., Molloy, G.N., Heyme, D., Murphy, G.C. and Ollendick, T. (1998) 'Emotive imagery treatment for childhood phobias: A credible and empirically validated intervention?' *Behavioural and Cognitive Psychotherapy, 26*, 103–113.

King, N.J., Ollendick, T.H. and Gullome, E. (1991) 'Test anxiety in children and adolescents.' *Australian Psychologist, 26*, 25–32.

Klein, J.B., Jacobs, R.H. and Reinecke, M.A. (2007) 'A meta-analysis of CBT in adolescents with depression.' *Journal of the American Academy of Child and Adolescent Psychiatry, 46*, 1403–1413.

Lewinsohn, P.M. and Clarke, G.N. (1999) 'Psychosocial treatments for adolescent depression.' *Clinical Psychology Review, 19*, 329–342.

McCaleb-Kahan, P. and Wenner, R. (2009) 'The relationship of student demographics to 10th grade MCAS test anxiety.' *NERA Conference Proceedings 2009*, Paper 27. Available at: http://digitalcommons.uconn.edu/nera_2009/27, accessed 23 November 2016.

McDonald, A.S. (2001) 'The prevalence and effects of test anxiety in school children.' *Educational Psychology, 21*, 89–101.

Mrazek, M.D., Franklin, M.S., Tarchin Phillips, D., Baird, B. and Schooler, J.W. (2013) 'Mindfulness training improves working memory capacity and GRE performance while reducing mind wandering.' *Psychological Science, 24*, 5, 776–781.

Murrell, A.R. and Scherbarth, A.J. (2006) 'State of the research and literature address: ACT with children, adolescents and parents.' *International Journal of Behavioral Consultation and Therapy, 2*, 4, 531–543.

National Institute for Health and Care Excellence (NICE) (2005a) 'Depression in children and young people: Identification and management in primary, community and secondary care.' *Clinical Guideline 28*. Available at: www.nice.org.uk/guidance/CG28, accessed 2 January 2013.

National Institute for Health and Care Excellence (NICE) (2005b) 'Obsessive-compulsive disorder: Core interventions in the treatment of obsessive compulsive disorder and body dysmorphic disorder.' *Clinical Guideline 31*. Available at: www.nice.org.uk/nicemedia/pdf/CG031niceguideline.pdf, accessed 2 January 2012.

Nie, Y., Lau, S. and Liau, A.K. (2011) 'Role of academic self-efficacy in moderating the relation between task importance and test anxiety.' *Learning and Individual Differences, 21*, 736–741.

NSPCC (2013) *Can I Tell You Something? ChildLine Review 2012–13.* London: NSPCC.

NSPCC (2014) *Under Pressure. ChildLine Review: What's Affected Children in April 2013–March 2014.* London: NSPCC.

NSPCC (2015a) *Always There When I Need You. ChildLine Review: What's Affected Children in April 2014–March 2015.* London: NSPCC.

NSPCC (2015b) as quoted in 'Turning exam stress into a positive', *SecEd*, 4 June 2015. Available at: www.sec-ed.co.uk/best-practice/turning-exam-stress-into-a-positive, accessed 23 November 2016.

NSPCC (2016) *Childline Annual Review 2015/16: It Turned Out Someone Did Care.* London: NSPCC.

O'Kearney, R.T., Anstey, K., von Sanden, C. and Hunt, A. (2006) 'Behavioural and cognitive behavioural therapy for obsessive compulsive disorder in children and adolescents.' *Cochrane Database of Systematic Reviews 2006*, Issue 4. Art. No.: CD004856. DOI:10.1002/14651858.CD004856.pub2. Published online January 2010.

Owens, M., Stevenson, J., Norgate, R. and Hadwin, J.A. (2008) 'Processing efficiency theory in children: Working memory as a mediator between test anxiety and academic performance.' *Anxiety, Stress and Coping, 21*, 417–430.

Owen-Yeates, A. (2005) 'Stress in Year 11 students.' *Pastoral Care in Education, 23*, 4, 42–51.

Pavlov, I.P. (1927) *Conditioned Reflexes: An Investigation of the Physiological Activity of the Cerebral Cortex.* Translated and edited by G.V. Anrep. London: Oxford University Press.

Putwain, D.W. (2007) 'Test anxiety in UK schoolchildren: Prevalence and demographic patterns.' *British Journal of Educational Psychology, 77*, 3, 579–593.

Putwain, D.W. (2008) 'Do high stakes examinations moderate the test anxiety–examination performance relationship?' *Educational Psychology, 28*, 2, 109–118.

Putwain, D.W. (2009) 'Situated and contextual features of test anxiety in UK adolescent students.' *School Psychology International, 30*, 56–74.

Putwain, D.W. and Best, N. (2011) 'Fear appeals in the primary classroom: Effects on test anxiety and test grade.' *Learning and Individual Differences, 21*, 580–584.

Putwain, D.W. and Best, N. (2012) 'Do highly test anxious students respond differentially to fear appeals made prior to a test?' *Research in Education*, 88, 1, 1–10.

Putwain, D.W. and Daniels, R.A. (2010) 'Is the relationship between competence beliefs and test anxiety influenced by goal orientation?' *Learning and Individual Differences, 20*, 1, 8–13.

Putwain, D.W. and Remedios, R. (2014) 'The scare tactic: Do fear appeals predict motivation and exam scores?' *School Psychology Quarterly, 29*, 4, 503–516.

Putwain, D.W. and Roberts, C.M. (2009) 'The development and validation of the Teachers Use of Fear Appeals Questionnaire.' *British Journal of Educational Psychology, 79*, 643–661.

Putwain, D.W. and Symes, W. (2011) 'Classroom fear appeals and examination performance: Facilitating or debilitating outcomes?' *Learning and Individual Differences, 21*, 227–232.

Putwain, D.W., Connors, L. and Symes, W. (2010) 'Do cognitive distortions mediate the test anxiety–examination performance relationship?' *Educational Psychology, 30*, 1, 11–26.

Putwain, D.W., Woods, K.A. and Symes, W. (2010) 'Personal and situational predictors of test anxiety of students in post-compulsory education.' *British Journal of Educational Psychology, 80*, 137–160.

Rapee, R.M., Wignall, A., Hudson, J.L. and Schniering, C.A. (2000) *Treating Anxious Children and Adolescents: An Evidence-Based Approach.* Oakland, CA: New Harbinger Publications.

Reiss, N., Warnecke, I., Tolgou, T., Krampen, D., Luka-Krausgrill, U. and Rohrmann, S. (2017) 'Effects of cognitive behavioural therapy with relaxation vs. imagery rescripting on text anxiety: A randomized controlled trial.' *Journal of Affective Disorders, 208*, 483–489.

Rosairio, P., Naez, J.C., Salgado, A., Gonzalez-Pienda, J.A. *et al.* (2008) 'Test anxiety: Associations with personal and family variables.' *Psicothema, 20*, 4, 563–570.

Scout Association (2007) as quoted in 'Teenagers under exam pressure', *The Metro*, January 2007. Available at: http://metro.co.uk/2007/01/07/teenagers-under-exam-pressure-514159, accessed 23 November 2016.

Segool, N. (2009) *Test Anxiety Associated with High-Stakes Testing among Elementary School Children: Prevalence, Predictors and Relationships to Student Performance*. Available at: http://gateway.proquest.com/openurl?url_ver=Z39.88-2004&rft_val_fmt=info:ofi/fmt:kev:mtx:dissertation&res_dat=xri:pqdiss&rft_dat=xri:pqdiss:3381350, accessed 10 July 2017.

Segool, N., Carlson, J., Goforth, A., von der Embse, N. and Barterian, J. (2013) 'Heightened test anxiety among young children: Elementary school students' anxious responses to high-stakes testing.' *Psychology in the Schools, 50*, 1, 489–499.

Sena, J.D.W., Lowe, P.A. and Lee, S.W. (2007) 'Significant predictors of test anxiety among students with and without learning disabilities.' *Journal of Learning Disabilities, 40*, 360–376.

Silverman, W.K., Kurtines, W.M., Ginsburg, G.S., Weems, C.F., Rabian, B. and Setafini, L.T. (1999) 'Contingency management, self-control and education support in the treatment of childhood phobic disorders: A randomized clinical trial.' *Journal of Consulting and Clinical Psychology, 67*, 675–687.

Skinner, B.F. (1938) *The Behavior of Organisms.* New York: Appleton-Century-Crofts.

Spence, S., Donovan, C. and Brechman-Toussaint, M. (2000) 'The treatment of childhood social phobia: The effectiveness of a social skills training-based cognitive behavioural intervention with and without parental involvement.' *Journal of Child Psychology and Psychiatry, 41*, 713–726.

Spielberger, C.D. (1980) *Preliminary Professional Manual for the Test Anxiety Inventory.* Palo Alto, CA: Consulting Psychologists Press.

The Prince's Trust (2013) *Abandoned Ambitions? The Need to Support Struggling School Leavers.* A report by The Prince's Trust, supported by HSBC. London: The Prince's Trust.

Tymms, P. and Merrell, C. (2007) *Standards and Quality in English Primary Schools Over Time.* Cambridge: University of Cambridge Faculty of Education.

von der Embse, N., Barterian, J. and Segool, N. (2013) 'Test anxiety interventions for children and adolescents: A systematic review of treatment studies from 2000–2010.' *Psychology in the Schools, 0*, 1–15.

Weems, C., Taylor, L., Costa, N., Marks, A. *et al.* (2009) 'Effect of a school-based test anxiety intervention in ethnic minority youth exposed to Hurricane Katrina.' *Journal of Applied Developmental Psychology, 30*, 218–226.

Wren, D.G. and Bensen, J. (2004) 'Measuring test anxiety on children: Scale development and internal construct validation.' *Anxiety, Stress and Coping, 17*, 227–240.

Young Researchers Dorset (2014) *Exam Stress.* Available at: www.dorsetyoungresearchers.com/gallery/exam%20stress%20report%20april%202014%20yp.pdf, accessed 12 December 2015.

Zeidner, M. and Mathews, G. (2005) 'Evaluation Anxiety.' In A.J. Elliot and C.S. Dweck (eds) *Handbook of Competence and Motivation.* London: Guilford Press.

'*Starving the Exam Stress Gremlin* meets a very real need given the increasing academic pressures on young people today. While there is plenty of advice out there about revision techniques, in my opinion, there is nothing so accessible, clear and well-researched about exam stress, its causes and ways to tackle it as this innovative workbook. My favourite thing is that *Starving the Exam Stress Gremlin* hands control back to young people – control over their own response to their exams – taking them on a journey from understanding to action. Unique, practical, humorous and warm; I would certainly recommend it to anyone whose exam stress is a barrier to success.'

– *Claire Tasker, Headteacher, High Storrs School, Sheffield*

'Another fantastic addition to the 'Starving the Gremlin' series. This series has been truly transformational – both for our young people and the adults who work with them. Kate has a way of making the most complex concepts of cognitive behavioural therapy understandable to all through a mix of written explanation, examples and creative illustration. Instantly usable, this latest workbook will be an invaluable resource for young people facing exams and for the adults helping them to prepare. A must read for anyone facing this situation or for those wanting to learn more about cognitive behavioural therapy in general and its impact on our emotions and behaviours.'

– *Rob Barraclough, Headteacher,*
St. Joseph's Catholic Primary School, Dewsbury

'In today's exam-led system, teaching the content of this unique book is, in my opinion, as important as teaching the subject content of the exam itself in order to create the positive conditions needed for mental wellbeing *and* academic success. Parents and professionals can also use the book's supportive techniques and reassuring phrases to encourage resilience, determination and a positive 'can do' approach from their child. As an emergency go-to or a step by step guide delivered over a period of time, this highly interactive workbook provides strategies to empower and take back control of the feelings which can challenge our ability to shine under test conditions. This book's accessible format transforms the science behind our 'Exam Stress Gremlins' into simple 'so what can I do about it?' guidance for lifelong success! Combining this with its easy to read style and use of stories and cartoons makes *Starving the Exam Stress Gremlin* a vital and memorable read!'

– *Vanessa Langley, Executive Headteacher, Gleadless*
and Arbourthorne Primary Federation, Sheffield

by the same author

Starving the Anxiety Gremlin
A Cognitive Behavioural Therapy Workbook on Anxiety Management for Young People
Kate Collins-Donnelly
ISBN 978 1 84905 341 9
eISBN 978 0 85700 673 8

Starving the Stress Gremlin
A Cognitive Behavioural Therapy Workbook on Stress Management for Young People
Kate Collins-Donnelly
ISBN 978 1 84905 340 2
eISBN 978 0 85700 672 1

Starving the Anger Gremlin
A Cognitive Behavioural Therapy Workbook on Anger Management for Young People
Kate Collins-Donnelly
ISBN 978 1 84905 286 3
eISBN 978 0 85700 621 9

Banish Your Body Image Thief
A Cognitive Behavioural Therapy Workbook on Building Positive Body Image for Young People
Kate Collins-Donnelly
ISBN 978 1 84905 463 8
eISBN 978 0 85700 842 8

Banish Your Self-Esteem Thief
A Cognitive Behavioural Therapy Workbook on Building Positive Self-Esteem for Young People
Kate Collins-Donnelly
ISBN 978 1 84905 462 1
eISBN 978 0 85700 841 1

of related interest

The Healthy Coping Colouring Book and Journal
Creative Activities to Help Manage Stress, Anxiety and Other Big Feelings
Pooky Knightsmith
Illustrated by Emily Hamilton
ISBN 978 1 78592 139 1
eISBN 978 1 78450 405 2

Set for Success
Activities for Teaching Emotional, Social and Organisational Skills
Josie Santomauro and Margaret Anne Carter
Illustrated by Carla Marino
ISBN 978 1 84905 058 6
eISBN 978 0 85700 244 0